Oregon

BLUE-RIBBON
Fly Fishing Guide

John Shewey

FRANK AMATO PHOTO

Oregon

BLUE-RIBBON
Fly Fishing Guide

John Shewey

Frank Amato
PORTLAND

ABOUT THE AUTHOR

A writer, author and photographer from Oregon, John Shewey travels extensively throughout the Northwest in pursuit of fly-angling adventures. Summer steelhead and upland gamebirds occupy much of his time during the autumn, but John's angling pursuits lead him annually to destinations ranging from the Pacific surf to the famous Western spring creeks to the the alpine lakes of the West. His steelhead flies have earned national recognition. John has authored numerous magazine articles and his other books include *Mastering the Spring Creeks, Fly Fishing for Summer Steelhead, Northwest Flyfishing: Trout & Beyond, Fly Fishing Pacific Northwest Waters, Alpine Angler,* and *North Umpqua Steelhead Journal.*

ACKNOWLEDGMENTS

This project would not have been possible if not for the assistance of many individuals. My sincere thanks go to the people of the Oregon Department of Fish & Wildlife, especially the following biologists: Wayne Bowers, Russ Stauff, Ted Fies, Steve Marx, Roger Smith, Walt Weber, John Spangler, Keith Braun, Rick Klumph, Wayne Hunt. Jim Cope of LaPine has my thanks for his contribution of beautifully tied lake flies, which appear in the fly plates. Thanks also to my fishing partners, Forrest Maxwell and Tim Blount, who have helped immensely in my "field research" (and loved every minute of it); finally, thanks to DeAnn for tolerating my many days afield each year.

Published in 1998 by:
Frank Amato Publications, Inc.
PO Box 82112 • Portland, Oregon 97282 • (503) 653-8108

Softbound ISBN: 1-57188-133-6 Softbound UPC: 0-66066-00333-1

Cover photo: Ken Morrish
Back Cover Photo: Dec Hogan
Fly Plates: Jim Schollmeyer
All other photographs taken by the author unless otherwise noted.

Book Design: Tony Amato
Cover design: Amy Tomlinson

Printed in Singapore

3 5 7 9 10 8 6 4 2

TABLE OF CONTENTS

Northwest

Astoria

28
27
26
22 23 24 25
21
18 19
17
16
15
14
13
12
11
10
9
8
7
4
5
6
3
2
1
20
29

Willamette

Portland

Salem

Eugene/Springfield

21
16
15
18
10
12
8
11
6
7
2
1
3

Northwest

Southwest

Coos Bay

Medford

15
5
7
8
2
11
6
3
9
10
4
2

Central

The Dalles

Klamath Falls

22
19 20
17
14
22
9
13
21
5
10 13
15 14
16 8 6
9
11 5
12
20
17
30
38
12
13 14
4

1
10
1
9
2
4
3
19 18
7

13 14
11 10
22
22
24
29
28
27
23
26
12
32
31
16
25

Nor

CENTRAL ZONE

1 Deschutes River (lower)
2 Metolius River
3 Crooked River
4 Deschutes River, Middle
5 Deschutes River, Upper
6 Upper Deschutes River
7 Little Deschutes River
8 Fall River
9 Crane Prairie Reservoir
10 Hosmer Lake
11 Wickiup Reservoir
12 Davis Lake
13 Sparks Lake
14 Lava Lake
15 Elk Lake
16 Cultus Lake & Little Cultis Lake
17 South Twin Lake
18 East Lake
19 Paulina Lake
20 Odell Lake
21 Suttle Lake
22 Hood River

SOUTHEAST ZONE

1 Mann Lake
2 Chickahominy Reservoir
3 Yellowjacket Lake
4 Delintment Lake
5 Malheur River System
6 Beulah Reservoir
7 Owyhee River
8 Blitzen River
9 Krumbo Reservoir
10 Ana River
11 Ana Reservoir
12 Chewaucan River
13 Thompson Valley Reservoir
14 Duncan Reservoir
15 Spaulding Reservoir
16 Deep Creek
17 Malheur Reservoir
18 Thief Valley Reservoir
19 Powder River
20 Anthony Lakes Area
21 Brownlee Reservoir
22 Williamson River
23 Sprague River
24 Sycan River
25 Klamath River
26 Upper Klamath Lake
27 Agency Lake
28 Wood River
29 Sevenmile Creek,
   Crooked Creek, Fort Creek
30 Miller Lake
31 Holbrook Reservoir
32 Cottonwood Meadows Lake

NORTHEAST ZONE

1 Grand Ronde River
2 Imnaha River
3 Minam River
4 Lostine River
5 Wallowa River
6 Wallowa Lake
7 Eagle Cap Wilderness
8 Wenaha River
9 John Day River
10 North Fork John Day River
11 Middle Fork John Day River
12 Umatilla River
13 Canyon Creek Meadows
   Reservoir (Canyon Meadows Lake)
14 Pilcher Creek Reservoir
15 Wolf Creek Reservoir

WILLAMETTE ZONE

1 McKenzie River
2 Willamette River (mainstem)
3 Middle Fork Willamette
4 Gold Lake
5 Lost Lake (Santiam Pass)
6 Mill Creek
7 South Santiam River
8 North Santiam River
9 North Santiam, Upper
10 Abiqua Creek
11 Breitenbush River
12 Silver Creek
13 Marion Lake
14 Round Lake
15 Clackamas River
16 Eagle Creek
17 Roaring River
18 Molalla River
19 Salmon River
20 Zigzag River
21 Sandy River
22 Willamette Zone High Lakes

NORTHWEST ZONE

1 Siuslaw River
2 Lake Creek
3 Big Creek, Rock Creek,
   Tenmile Creek, Bob's Creek
4 Alsea River
5 Five Rivers
6 Lobster Creek
7 Drift Creek (Alsea tributary)
8 Beaver Creek
9 Siletz River
10 Drift Creek
11 Salmon River
12 Nestucca River
13 Little Nestucca River
14 Three Rivers
15 Tillamook River
16 Trask River
17 Wilson River
18 Kilchis River
19 Miami River
20 Salmonberry River
21 North Fork Nehalem River
22 Nehalem River
23 Cook Creek
24 Rock Creek
25 Humbug Creek
26 Necanicum River
27 Klaskanine River
28 Young's River
29 Clatskanie River

SOUTHWEST ZONE

1 North Umpqua
2 Rogue River
3 Illinois River
4 Applegate River
5 Coquille River
6 Pistol River
7 Sixes River
8 Elk River
9 Chetco River
10 Winchuk River
11 Hunter Creek
12 Diamond Lake
13 Lemolo Lake
14 Toketee Reservoir
15 Mainstem Umpqua River

MAP   7

KEN MORRISH PHOTO

INTRODUCTION

In writing this guide book, I had to consider many potential consequences. Chief among these is the fact that by virtue of writing about specific destinations I would likely make somebody mad. After all, none of us likes to see our "pet" waters written up in either book or magazine form. My answer to that was simply to focus on the most significant waters—those waters of most interest to fly anglers. In the case of small waters in out-of-the-way places, I decided in many cases to offer enough comment to get you started in the right direction. For other such waters, I have said little or nothing: Anyone with a desire to explore new places can locate a tiny mountain stream or a remote alpine lake on a Forest Service map, lace up the hiking boots, and embark on a voyage of discovery. You don't need my help to do that.

I have not visited every destination listed in this book. I have fished most of them. Those places to which I have not personally ventured, however, received the same thorough research as those places with which I am familiar. My goal, above all else, was to write an accurate and useful guide to the many great trout and steelhead waters in Oregon, the state that I have called home for two decades.

Within this guide, I hope you will find information that will help you discover Oregon from a fly-angler's perspective. Writing this book was a great experience for me as I visited waters I have always wanted to fish and re-acquainted myself with old stomping grounds, re-kindling fond memories of great days afield. There can be little doubt that Oregon is among the truly great fly-angling states, for it offers world-class trout fishing and anadromous fish in relative abundance. With this guide in hand and a willingness to explore, I think you will discover why so many fly anglers call Oregon home.

CENTRAL ZONE

The Central Zone in Oregon offers a combination of all the best that Oregon has to offer the fly angler. The Deschutes River runs south to north through the entire region and is the state's best combination trout and summer steelhead stream in its lower 100 miles. The Metolius, Crooked and Fall rivers are among the state's most popular trout-fishing destinations. Added to this rich diversity of stream fishing are the productive lakes near "Century Drive" east and southeast of Bend. These include famed waters like Crane Prairie Reservoir, Hosmer Lake and Davis Lake.

The landscape is equally diverse in this region, ranging from the snow-capped flanks of the volcanic peaks in the Cascade Range to the broad sagebrush desert steppe on the east edge of the Central Zone. In between are lush ponderosa stands, magnificent desert canyons and some scenic, isolated ranges such as the Paulina Mountains and Ochoco Mountains.

The climate, of course, is equally diverse and its severity is more-or-less altitude dependent. One-hundred-degree days make the Lower Deschutes a miserable place during July and August, but the same weather offers the most perfect of conditions on the many high lakes of the Three Sisters or Mt. Jefferson Wilderness areas. Winter brings an end to the lake fishing, but the popular rivers—Deschutes, Metolius and Crooked—offer excellent "off-season" fishing, including some dry-fly fishing.

An abundance of excellent waters makes the Central Zone a destination for countless fly anglers. Thus crowded conditions are not uncommon during the peak season on places like Hosmer Lake, Crane Prairie, the Metolius and the Lower Deschutes. Those who seek solitude and good fishing will do well to fish these waters mid-week or early and late in the season.

Another way to escape the crowds is to fish out-of-the-way waters, both streams and lakes. I have chosen in this book not to write about the upper forks of the Crooked River or backcountry lakes of the Taylor Burn area, yet these places, and many others, offer enjoyable fishing for small trout in an atmosphere of near total solitude. The price is paid in getting there, for the region's least crowded waters are those requiring backcountry drives over long gravel roads and/or cross-country hikes through the Cascades or Ochocos.

Given the popularity and productivity of the numerous top-flight fisheries in Central Oregon, it should come as no surprise that a number of fly shops do a strong business in the area. As of this writing, Bend offers three fly shops, Sunriver, two, and one each in Sisters, Camp Sherman and Maupin. Also as of this writing, all these shops are run by quality owners and employees and for that reason alone I hesitate to recommend one over the others, but each offers its unique aspects.

By a combination of its exceptional destination fisheries and its strong fly-angling community, Oregon's Central Region essentially defines fly fishing in the state.

Mouth of the Deschutes where it enters the Columbia River.

FRANK AMATO PHOTO

Dangerous rapids must be carefully negotiated by boats.

Deschutes River (Lower)

The Lower Deschutes, Oregon's premier trout and summer steelhead stream, gouges out a deep desert canyon on its tumultuous 100-mile journey from Pelton Dam to the Columbia River. A dozen major rapids, and many minor ones, roar through this canyon, whose steep rimrock-lined walls reach as high as 2,000 feet above the river.

The Deschutes is truly a gem, for few, if any, other rivers can boast of both a blue-ribbon trout fishery and a superb summer steelhead fishery. The river's trout, called "redsides" because of their coloration, are abundant throughout most of the river. They commonly exceed a foot in length, with 13- to 16-inch fish being typical. Redsides of 17 to 20 inches are fairly common, though not necessarily easy to catch.

For quite a number of years now, angling from a floating device has been prohibited on the Deschutes. Virtually all fly anglers who frequent the river agree that this one law has preserved the quality of the trout fishery despite ever-growing numbers of people. This regulation prevents people from floating down the river and pounding away at every likely spot from the front of a drift boat. Many of the hard-to-reach areas harbor big trout—often substantial numbers of big trout. Only the creative wader and brush-buster will hook these fish.

In fact, some of the best dry-fly fishing on the Deschutes occurs when pods of trout begin rising in large back-eddies and under lush overhanging tree branches. Again, a well-planned approach coupled with accurate presentation will typically be rewarded.

The Deschutes offers many excellent hatches between April and October. The first major hatch, and the most significant of the season in terms of the reaction it inspires among anglers, is the famed stonefly hatch of late May and June.

From Warm Springs, just a few miles below the impoundment that separates the massive Lower Deschutes from her diminutive upriver sources (the Middle and Upper Deschutes), to the town of Maupin some 50 miles below, the Deschutes is famed for its hatches of giant stoneflies (salmonflies) and golden stoneflies. Anglers from all over converge on this section of river to fish the stoneflies. Less pressured, the lower river, downstream of Maupin offers the same dense emergence of stoneflies. The hatch works its way upriver as water temperatures rise.

At the same time, blue-winged olive (*Baetis*) and pale morning dun (*Ephemerella*) mayflies emerge, along with increasingly dense caddis activity, the latter being especially profuse in the evenings. Localized, sporadic hatches of green drakes (*Drunella*) often occur on cloudy, blustery days during the stonefly period.

By early July, the stonefly carnival is over. Caddis now dominate the hatch scene and will continue to do so throughout the summer and fall, although several mayflies offer fishable and sometimes heavy hatches along certain stretches of river. Pale morning duns and blue-winged olives are chief among these, but mahogany duns (*Paraleptophlebia*) and green

Whitehorse Rapids.

Good trout and steelhead water above Maupin.

Deschutes River Steelhead

Between August and early November, summer steelhead stack up in all the good holding water throughout the river. These are a mix of several steelhead: Wild, native Deschutes River fish, hatchery steelhead and strays—both wild and hatchery-origin—from other rivers, especially Idaho streams. Most will weigh five to eight pounds; many will reach 12 pounds and a few monsters of 14 to 18 pounds fall to fly anglers each season. Hot fish are the rule. They use the huge river and its strong currents to good advantage.

They respond readily to dry-line tactics, at least when the sun is off the water. Because the river runs south to north, the fish must look directly into the sun during the day. Perhaps they simply can't see flies swimming near the surface when the glare from the sun obscures the upward view. Mid- to late autumn brings short days and many overcast ones along with a lower sun. All-day fishing is often possible. Nonetheless, August and September are the big months for Deschutes River steelhead anglers.

Naturally, the early action—July and August—is concentrated in the lower end of the river, especially the 25-mile reach from Macks Canyon to the mouth. Although one rough road leads into the canyon at a railroad site called Kloan, some eight miles up from the mouth, I hesitate to recommend this option: Should you wish to proceed during summer, I suggest scouting the road before traveling in your four-wheel-drive vehicle; should you wish to proceed during mid- to late fall, I'd suggest putting your affairs in order.

The better three options are all quite popular: 1. Hire a jet-boat guide and fish from the mouth of the river up. 2. Float from Macks Canyon to

Male steelhead from lower part of the river.

drakes offer highly localized hatches during different times of the summer and early fall. The best of these mayfly hatches usually coincide with those precious few overcast summer days.

Of summertime caddis hatches, there are many. *Rhyacophila* (green rock worm) and *Hydropsyche* (tan spotted sedge) are abundant throughout the river, but so too are many others. Rather than focus on specific caddis species, anglers would be well-served to carry a variety of patterns in sizes 12 through 18. The Deschutes offers every imaginable type of water: deep, gliding runs, expansive riffles, shallow tailouts, boulder-studded pocket water, swirling eddies and everything else. Caddis patterns should match the water type: X-Caddis or Elk Hair Caddis for choppy water; sparse X-Caddis or spent-wing caddis patterns for smooth water. In fact, anglers who switch to spring-creek-type patterns and tactics when fishing the flat-water parts of the Deschutes invariably bring more trout to the dry fly than those who simply throw an Elk Hair Caddis at every rise.

Aside from the "splash-and-giggle" crowd, whose endless array of inflatables parade downriver on weekends, the Deschutes can be a quiet place during the height of summer, when July days bring scorching temperatures, relentless sun and an indomitable daytime wind. Anglers willing to brave all of the above and/or concentrate their efforts during the very early morning and evening hours will often find long stretches of river empty of other anglers.

By August, steelhead have entered the river in good numbers and the guides are working the lower end of the river—the 25-mile stretch from the mouth of the Deschutes up to Macks Canyon. Caddis activity continues for trout anglers, but by late August and September the focus for many shifts to steelhead.

Suckers will on rare occasion take a dry fly meant for trout.

Wild steelhead.

the mouth, a stretch that will take you through several serious rapids. 3. Walk or bike up from the mouth on either bank, with the east bank being the better choice for bikers because you follow the fairly level service road. Likewise, you can hike down from Macks Canyon along the east bank, although it is not particularly easy going.

By late August or early September, steelhead have passed Sherar's Falls (17 miles upstream from Macks Canyon) in sufficient numbers to warrant fishing the rest of the Deschutes, from Sherar's all the way to Warm Springs. The reach from Macks Canyon up to Sherar's Falls is a popular stretch owing to the abundance of good water and to the rough gravel access road that parallels the river for the entire distance. The next eight miles (Sherar's up to Maupin) are paralleled by a paved road and another six miles of gravel takes you to the "Locked Gate" above Maupin. Only foot traffic is allowed above Locked Gate.

Covering the water effectively is more important than worrying over particular fly patterns. Standard Deschutes River favorites include the Skunk, Green-butt Skunk, Freight Train and Macks Canyon. I rely on the latter fly along with the Rick's Revenge and Spawning Purple for most of my fishing. An eight- or nine-weight rod will handle the wind and the strong fish and will allow for long casts over big water. In addition, don't leave home without cleated wading boots. The Deschutes is notorious for treacherous wading.

The Deschutes, like many Northwest rivers, has inspired its share of steelhead patterns. Among the most popular is Doug Stewart's 1972 invention called the Max Canyon or Macks Canyon. Randall Kaufmann's Freight Train, Signal Light and Coal Car are more recently developed favorites, all borrowing the idea of a bright butt and a dark-colored body.

Max Canyon (Doug Stewart)

Tag: Flat gold tinsel, optional
Tail: Orange and white mixed (calf tail in the original, but hackle fibers are now popular)
Butt: Orange wool
Body: Black wool, chenille or dubbing
Rib: Gold
Hackle: Black
Wing: White with orange over top; calf tail or similar

Black Max (Shewey, et al)

Tag: Flat gold tinsel
Tail: Orange-dyed golden pheasant crest
Butt: Orange wool
Body: Black wool
Rib: Gold oval
Hackle: Black
Wing: Black bear
Cheeks: Jungle cock

Stewart (Marty Sherman)

Tag: Flat gold tinsel
Tail: Golden pheasant tippet fibers
Rib: Gold
Body: Black wool
Collar: Soft black hackle
Wing: Black calf tail with a sparse bunch of orange calf tail over

Deschutes Special (Mike Kennedy)

Tail: Red hackle fibers
Body: Fluorescent green floss
Rib: Small silver oval
Hackle: Dun gray
Wing: Gray squirrel tail
Cheeks: Jungle cock

Deschutes Demon (Don McClain)

Tail: Hot orange hackle fibers or dyed golden pheasant crest
Body: Gold wool
Rib: Embossed gold tinsel
Hackle: Hot orange
Wing: Brown deer body hair with white bucktail over

Deschutes Skunk (Lola McClain)

Tail: Red hackle fibers
Body: Black wool
Rib: Embossed silver tinsel
Hackle: Black
Wing: Brown deer body hair with white bucktail over

Patriot (Frank Amato)

Tail:	Red hackle fibers
Body:	Yellow floss
Rib:	Flat silver tinsel
Hackle:	Deep purple
Wing:	White

Night Dancer (Frank Amato)

Tail:	Red hackle fibers
Body:	Black floss
Rib:	Flat silver tinsel
Hackle:	Deep purple
Wing:	Black

Rick's Revenge (John Shewey/Rick Wren)

Tag:	Flat silver tinsel
Tail:	Fluorescent hot pink floss
Butt:	Fluorescent hot pink floss veiled above with strands of same
Body:	Purple dubbing ribbed with fine silver oval
Hackle:	Purple
Wing:	White with purple over
Collar:	Purple-dyed guinea
Cheeks:	Jungle cock

Patricia (Randy Stetzer)

Tag:	Fine oval gold tinsel, optional
Tail:	Claret hackle fibers
Body:	Claret seal or Angora dubbing
Rib:	Gold oval tinsel
Hackle:	Claret
Wing:	White
Cheeks:	Jungle cock
Head:	Claret

Freight Train (Randall Kaufmann)

Tail:	Purple hackle tips or dyed golden pheasant crest
Butt:	1/2 fluorescent orange floss or wool, 1/2 fluorescent red floss or wool
Body:	Purple chenille or dubbing
Rib:	Silver oval
Hackle:	Purple
Wing:	White

Coal Car (Randall Kaufmann)

Tail:	Black hackle fibers
Butt:	1/2 fluorescent red-orange yarn or floss, 1/2 fluorescent red yarn or floss
Body:	Black chenille
Hackle:	Black
Wing:	Black with a few strands of black Krystal Flash

Trout

Perhaps the easiest way not to catch steelhead on the Deschutes is to allow the trout to get to you. That magical evening steelhead time arrives when the sun is well off the water and the dusk is gathering. As you cast your way through a steelhead run, you start hearing the rises. Trout. Big ones.

Caddisflies appear in droves, smallish types at first, but soon joined by the big October caddis, whose inch-long orange bodies demand size 6 imitations. Caddis are everywhere and the trout are going nuts and you're hoping for one or two steelhead. This is the time that separates the species—separates the true-blue, die-hard steelheaders from the avid dry-fly trout fanatics—for only the dedicated steelhead angler can ignore the antics of Deschutes River rainbows, many from 14 to 18 inches, rising freely for caddis adults and porpoising in hot pursuit of emerging caddis pupae.

Autumn trout-fishing can be fast and furious on the Lower Deschutes. Evenings are usually best, but morning and midday brings caddis flights and localized blue-winged olive hatches. The "redsides" as these colorful, native Deschutes rainbows are called, inhabit the river in abundance and are managed to promote healthy wild populations.

They are an exceptional breed of rainbow, strong, heavy and full of fight. They take dry flies well during the hatches and even during non-hatch periods, anglers who fish the foam-lines, back-eddies and tree-canopied edges will find free-rising trout. In fact, the "combat anglers," who fight the dense shoreline shrubbery and wade the difficult-to-reach eddies and foamlines are often rewarded with 16- to 20-plus-inch rainbows. Nymphers will delight in the effectiveness of small nymphs drifted through the riffles.

Despite the exceptional trout-fishing in the fall, the crowds of stonefly time are but a distant memory and trout fanatics need only share the water with steelheaders. That situation requires comment, for trout anglers working up through a pool are in natural conflict with steelheaders moving down through the same water. Tradition and common courtesy dictate that the trout angler recognize that steelheaders intend to fish out the pool; and that steelhead anglers ask before entering a pool occupied by trout anglers or other steelheaders.

Steelhead are the reason for my autumn visits to the Deschutes, but the rising trout are always a serious temptation. Sometimes I get the best of both worlds by casting over steelhead water until the sun creeps over the canyon rim and then filling my afternoon with trout-fishing until the

Rainbow trout.

JIM SCHOLLMEYER PHOTO

Dave Stone fishing for trout.

sun disappears behind the massive rimrocks.

This is a comfortable pattern but one that lasts only a scant month or two each season. Indeed I wish we had more Octobers every year.

By far the most popular time for Deschutes River trout-fishing is the late spring/early summer period when the stoneflies emerge. Salmonflies (*Pteronarcys*) hatch first, usually appearing on the lower river by mid-May. The hatch progresses upriver and reaches the upper waters by late May or early June. The golden stoneflies follow in quick succession and the typical day in early June offers both salmonflies and golden stoneflies. They cling to the shoreline vegetation during the day but fly out over the water to deposit egg clusters during late afternoon and evening.

During this same period, hatches of several mayflies begin: pale morning duns (*Ephemerella*) and pale evening duns (*Heptagenia*) are the most important during the stonefly period, and cloudy, cool days usually offer strong hatches. Many trout, especially those that have been pounded by stonefly imitations, prefer the PMDs over the larger bugs. Blue-winged olives can hatch this time of year as well, as do Western green drakes (*Drunella*). Green drakes hatch sporadically on cool, overcast days, but it doesn't take too many of these big mayflies to get trout interested.

The blue-winged olive (*Baetis*) hatches can occur just about any time and with varying degrees of intensity. Hatches of pale evening duns and mahogany duns can prompt good rises from time to time between midsummer and early autumn, but neither is predictable in venue, timing or intensity.

As mentioned previously, caddis dominate the summer hatch scene, with most of the action compressed toward morning and evening. The October caddis joins the parade any time between mid-September and early November. These big orange insects offer a substantial meal for the trout, but the emergences are unpredictable and irregular. You can't count on the hatch but when it occurs, you'll long remember the experience.

Trout-fishing begins anew early in the spring: The lower river, downstream from the Warm Springs Reservation, is (as of this writing) open all year for trout fishing. Hatches of Chironomids (midges) and *Baetis* mayflies provide surface action on warm days as early as February; Western March browns appear late February or mid-April, depending on weather patterns and on specific locations. Winter/spring dry-fly angling can be highly productive at times, with much depending on water levels and weather. Expect the hatches to come off around midday.

Deschutes River Access

Access to the Deschutes River is difficult in sections. The upper end of the river is bordered by the Warm Springs Indian Reservation for about 30 miles. Within the reservation boundaries, the west bank to mid-river is strictly off limits except for a six-mile reach from Dry Creek Campground down to the opposite bank from Trout Creek Campground. Anglers fishing this stretch must obtain a tribal permit (also to camp at Dry Creek).

Floating anglers can drift the easy stretch from Warm Springs down to Trout Creek and find lots of trout-filled water. This float covers almost 10 miles. Beyond Trout Creek (which offers a large campground), the river travels almost 30 miles to the next good take-out at the little town of Maupin. Only experienced boaters should float this section, which includes the famous three-mile-long Whitehorse Rapids (class IV) as well as other major rapids, including Buckskin Mary and Boxcar.

A mile and a half below Warm Springs is a popular campground called Mecca Flat, accessed by dirt road just off the east end of the Warm Springs Bridge. Good river trails follow the Deschutes from Mecca to Trout Creek, providing access to more than seven miles of prime water.

The only drive-in access between Trout Creek and Maupin is South Junction, reached via Hwy. 97 north of Madras. South Junction access covers about 1.5 miles of public water.

A caddis imitation fooled this fish.

JIM SCHOLLMEYER PHOTO

The eight-mile reach from Maupin (pop. 500, all services) to Sherar's Falls (impassable) is home to one of the state's greatest splash-and-giggle circuses during the summer as raft-rental outfits do a booming business. This stretch does offer lots of good trout and steelhead water. A rough gravel road leads about 7 miles upriver from Maupin on the east bank before ending at the Locked Gate. Walk-in traffic is allowed beyond the gate. There is lots of good steelhead and trout water above Maupin and less raft traffic once you get above popular Harpham Flats.

Below Sherar's Falls, a rough gravel road parallels most of the 17 miles of river down to Macks Canyon, where a large campground attracts steelheaders during late summer and fall.

The remaining 25 miles from Macks Canyon to the mouth is accessed primarily by floating down or jet-boating up. Hikers and mountain bikers can travel the east bank up from the mouth where an old railroad grade is maintained as a service road for about 21 miles. Most of this area is easy going. The first few miles below Macks Canyon are quite the opposite. This lower 25 miles is popular and productive steelhead water and first-timers might consider hiring one of the numerous guides who specialize in steelheading the lower river.

A few notes: Boaters and their passengers need to obtain a boater's permit (available at fly shops and outdoor stores in the region); you will also need a Warm Springs Tribal Permit to fish the reservation side of the river where allowed. Carry your own water as only a few campsites offer drinking water. Some people voice concern over rattlesnakes that reside along the river, but you could easily go years without ever seeing one. If snakes bother you, keep your eyes peeled; if not, don't give them a second thought. Wear cleated wading boots.

Deschutes River Hatches

STONEFLIES	TIME	PATTERNS
Golden Stonefly (*Hesperoperla*)	May-June	Size 6-8
		Maxwell's Jughead, yellow
		Yellow Stimulator
		golden stonefly nymphs
Giant Stonefly "Salmonfly" (*Pteronarcys californica*)	May-June	Size 4-6
		Maxwell's Jughead, orange
		Orange Stimulator
		Bird's Stone
		Brook's Stonefly Nymph
		Kaufmann Stone Nymph, size 2-6
Little Yellow Stonefly	June-July	Size 10-14
		Quigley Yellow Sally
		Maxwell's Jughead, yellow

CADDISFLIES	TIME	PATTERNS
Green Sedge (*Rhyacophila*)	May-August	Size 14
		Elk Hair Caddis, green
		X-Caddis, green
		Green Rockworm
Short-horned Sedge "Saddle-Case Caddis" (*Glossosoma*)	May-Sept.	Size 16-18
		Elk Hair Caddis, tan
		X-Caddis, tan
		Spent Caddis
Spotted Sedge (*Hydropsyche*)	May-Aug.	Size 12-14
		Elk Hair Caddis, tan
		X-Caddis, tan
		Spent Caddis, tan
		CDC Caddis Adult, tan
Little Western Weedy Water Sedge (*Amiocentrus aspilus*)	May-July	Size 16-18
		"Little Green Sedge"
		Elk Hair Caddis, green
		X-Caddis, green
		CDC Sparkle Emerger, green
October Caddis (*Dicosmoecus*)	Late Sept./Oct.	Size 6-8
		Orange Stimulator
		Maxwell's Jughead, orange
Micro-caddis (several genera)	May-Oct.	Size 20-22
		X-Caddis
		Spent-wing Caddis

MAYFLIES	TIME	PATTERNS
Blue-winged Olive (*Baetis*)	Year-round; best Mar.-May and Oct-Nov	Size 18-22
		Sparkle Dun
		Floating Nymph
		CDC Baetis Emerger
Pale Morning Dun (*Ephemerella inermis*)	May-July	Size 14-16
		PMD Sparkle Dun
		PMD CDC Emerger
		PMD CDC Dun
Western March Brown (*Rhithrogena morrisoni*)	March-April	Size 12-14
		Sparkle Dun, tan
		CDC Dun, tan
Western Green Drake (*Drunella*)	May-June rainy days; sparse & inconsistent	Size 10
		Lawson Paradrake
		Sparkle Dun
Slate-winged Olive (*Drunella coloradensis*)	June-July	Size 12-14
		Sparkle Dun, medium green
		Emergent Cripple
		CDC Dun
Mahogany Dun (*Paraleptophlebia*)	September	Size 16
		Emergent Cripple, brown
		Sparkle Dun, brown
		CDC Dun, brown
Pale Evening Dun (*Heptagenia*)	June-July	Size 14
		Sparkle Dun, pale yellow-tan
		CDC Emerger, pale yellow-tan
		Emergent Cripple, pale yellow-tan

Metolius River

Among Oregon's most popular fly-fishing destinations, the Metolius River is a spring creek that gouges out a wide, forested canyon northwest of the little town of Sisters. Consistently cold, clear waters and a canopy of ponderosa pines and other conifers make the Metolius a unique and attractive setting. With stocking of hatchery-reared rainbow trout discontinued in 1996, it is hoped that the river's wild redband rainbows will thrive in a stream now managed for wild fish.

The Metolius is a classic spring creek in every respect, save one: Unlike the famous spring creeks of Idaho and other locales, the Metolius is a medium- and high-gradient stream, lacking the slow, smooth sections that fly anglers generally associate with spring creeks. Thus the Metolius combines elements of both spring creeks and freestone rivers: Its mayfly hatches can be dense, yet golden stoneflies and October caddis are abundant as well.

In addition to rainbows that commonly span 10 to 16 inches and sometimes exceed 20 inches, the Metolius is home to a fairly dense population of bull trout, some of which reach 10 pounds or more. These bull trout have been eager predators of the hatchery trout planted in the river for decades, but the river's populations of whitefish, sculpin, kokanee and trout assure that the bull trout won't go hungry.

With the stocking of hatchery-reared trout no longer practiced on the Metolius, the density of trout is down considerably. ODFW estimates that the wild redband trout inhabit the river at less than 100 fish per mile, with the great majority of these being juvenile trout less than nine inches in length. The Metolius' steep gradient, cold temperatures and relative lack of cover simply do not allow for large trout densities. ODFW and anglers alike hope that the absence of hatchery trout can open additional habitat for native redbands, allowing densities to increase. This won't happen quickly, nor will a dramatic increase in fish numbers occur.

Hence the Metolius of the future will likely be a river where devout fly anglers must work diligently to find large wild trout. Anglers who switch to spring-creek tactics (downstream presentation, long tippets,

sparse flies) and who explore the river's more remote reaches, will likely be rewarded from time to time with a 16- to 20-inch redband.

The upper reaches of the Metolius are fly-only (Lake Creek down to Bridge 99). From Bridge 99 down to Lake Billy Chinook, the river is fly/artificial lure water. Throughout, trout must be released and angling from a floating device is prohibited.

The upper third of the Metolius, from Lake Creek to Bridge 99, offers mostly easy access along the roads and near the campgrounds. Trails follow the river and also lead to the river from where the roads swing away to the east. Below Bridge 99, access is by a rugged dirt/rock road that parallels the river for more than 10 miles. Don't start down this road with a full cup of coffee because you'll be wearing most of it within 50 yards. Those who don't mind having their fillings jolted loose will find these middle reaches of the Metolius to be lightly fished. Fast water predominates, so you must walk between pools and other good trout cover, but the fishing down here is often better than in the crowded campground waters above.

Metolius River.

FRANK AMATO PHOTO

Metolius River downstream from Camp Sherman.

The lower end of the Metolius is equally devoid of anglers. You can reach the lower river and its mouth at the Metolius Arm of Lake Billy Chinook from either the south or the east. From Hwy. 20 west of Sisters, turn north at Indian Ford Campground and follow Forest Primary Route 11 past Black Butte, down the Fly Creek drainage and eventually to its junction with FR1170. Follow 1170 as it snakes down to the Metolius Arm. From the east, along Hwy. 97 about halfway between Madras and the Crooked River Bridge, watch for signs announcing Cove Palisades State Park. Turn west and head for Cove Palisades, where you will cross first the Crooked River Arm and then the Deschutes Arm of Lake Billy Chinook. Continue west on this road (Route 64) until you reach the Metolius Arm.

Monty Campground is located at the mouth of the river on the western end of the Metolius Arm. Another brutally rough road leads up the river for about five miles. The end of this road is only two miles or so from the end of the dirt road leading downstream from Bridge 99 and the two are connected by trail.

Campgrounds are located all along the upper river and several private resorts offer nice accommodations in the vicinity of Camp Sherman. The Camp Sherman Store offers all the necessary amenities, including a fly shop.

Summer on the upper river offers nice weather and lots of people, along with good hatches of caddis and golden stoneflies. The middle and lower reaches, below Bridge 99 are largely deserted except by the handful of adventurous types looking to escape the crowds. During winter, the river is open downstream from Allingham Bridge (located below Camp Sherman). Most of the winter action is on nymphs but an occasional hatch of midges, blue-winged olives or winter stoneflies can stir trout to rise during the afternoon.

Mt. Jefferson looms above the Head of the Metolius.

Crooked River

Meandering through a spectacular desert canyon for much of its length, the Crooked River is beautiful in every aspect save the water itself, which flows perpetually off-color because of its source: A sediment-laden bottom-feed from Bowman Dam, which backs up sprawling Prineville Reservoir.

Despite the muddy water, the Crooked River offers some of the finest year-round fly angling in Central Oregon. The river's rainbow trout offer several fine qualities in that they are abundant, aggressive and they respond fairly well to good hatches. What they lack is size. Three out of four isn't bad.

Most of the trout will run eight to 12 inches. Trout from 12 to 20 inches are available and fly anglers take quite a few of these larger fish every season. In fact, two or three stable-flow years in a row generally equates to more large fish and a better average size.

The first 10 or 12 miles below Bowman Dam are most popular with fly anglers, but various sections farther downriver offer excellent angling and more solitude. The Crooked River Gorge area is among these. A steep climb into this awesome canyon keeps most folks out; those who make the trek are often rewarded with excellent fishing all to themselves.

The gorge section flows through quite a lot of private property so access can be a problem. The easiest entrance to the gorge is through the access at Opal Springs south of the little town of Culver (off Hwy. 97). Anglers must check in at the Opal Springs office before driving through on the road, which is open on weekdays. Weekenders will have to park at the rim and hike a little over a mile into the canyon. Adventurous anglers with good maps (Central Oregon Public Lands, available from BLM and USGS topos) can locate the other access areas between Smith Rock State Park (east of Hwy. 97) and the downstream end of the Gorge. Be prepared to knock on doors to get permission from landowners.

The Crooked River downstream from Bowman Dam perpetually flows off-color.

The stretch of river flowing through Smith Rock State Park offers reasonable fishing—sometimes downright good fishing when heavy summer caddis activity erupts during late evening and very early morning. Despite its immense popularity with rock climbers, Smith Rock rarely suffers from crowds of anglers. The park is a fee area so bring some dollar bills and bring a camera, for Smith Rock offers some of Central Oregon's most spectacular vistas.

The rainbows in the Crooked respond eagerly to early and late-season hatches of blue-winged olives, Chironomids and caddis. Summer rises are largely confined to early morning and late evening when caddis activity can bring trout-laden pools to a boil. In the absence of substantial hatches, Crooked River trout tend to be bottom-oriented. In the stretch below Bowman Dam, any variety of nymphs will work. Try Hare's Ears, Pheasant Tails and scuds any time of year.

The Crooked River is a popular winter destination for fly anglers because the releases from Bowman Dam keep the stream at a fairly constant flow and temperature until the spring thaw begins in the Ochoco Mountains and Maury Mountains. Chironomid hatches are common; blue-winged olive hatches begin during early spring and re-appear during autumn.

During the summer, dry-fly enthusiasts should look for areas of deep shade, where a few rising trout can typically be found. Otherwise, be prepared with caddis pupae patterns, which frequently outfish caddis dries (although the latter can be highly productive late evening and early morning).

Wet-wading may seem like a good idea during a 90-degree summer day when you fish the stretch below Bowman Dam, but the water is surprisingly cold. If you go waderless, wear a pair of felt-soled or cleated wading boots. A phone call to one of Central Oregon's myriad fly shops should precede any venture to the Crooked, especially during winter and spring when the water might be roaring through the canyon, making the river totally unfishable.

Deschutes River, Middle
(Bend to Lake Billy Chinook)

Naturally reproducing brown trout are the featured attraction throughout most of the Middle Deschutes, which flows some 50 miles between Bend and Lake Billy Chinook to the north.

The Middle Deschutes is another of Central Oregon's popular winter fisheries. Summer flows are severely reduced by a massive irrigation draw, but when the irrigation season ends and the water is channeled back to the river, the Middle Deschutes triples in size, allowing pool-bound trout to spread out.

What's more, the Middle Deschutes offers a very reliable February hatch of winter stoneflies (little brown stones or little black stones of the Family Nemouridae). These small (size 12-18) stoneflies emerge during the warmest part of the day, typically between noon and 3 p.m., and a 45-degree day during mid-February can bring swarms of the insects out for trout to prey upon. The stoneflies bring trout to the surface, offering anglers an opportunity to fish dry flies during winter.

Popular and accessible reaches of the Middle Deschutes include the area in the immediate vicinity of Lower Bridge (follow Lower Bridge Road west from its intersection with Hwy. 97 north of Terrebonne), the Folly Waters area and Steelhead Falls stretch (also accessed via Lower Bridge Road; turn off at the Crooked River Ranch Road and take a good map), Tetherow Crossing, Odin Falls and Cline Falls Park, the latter three sites all between Tumalo and Hwy. 126.

Anglers looking for an adventure can make the trek into the lower canyon, below the confluence with Squaw Creek. Just above Lake Billy Chinook, several miles of difficult-access public land envelopes the canyon, which by the time it reaches Squaw Creek has become a deep, massive affair. This lower reach of the Middle Deschutes offers solitude, brown trout, rainbow trout, whitefish and bull trout (which must be released unharmed).

From fall through mid-spring, the Middle Deschutes flows high and offers several good hatches.

Forrest Maxwell hooked this nice Middle Deschutes brown trout on a little black stonefly pattern.

Favorite flies to match the winter stoneflies include the Black Elk Hair Caddis, Floatin Fool and Black Quigley Stone. Spring brings hatches of blue-winged olive mayflies, March brown mayflies, brown willow flies (a variety of golden stonefly), pale morning duns, various caddis and salmonflies. All of these hatches can be highly localized.

Depending on a particular year's water supply, the Middle Deschutes will be sucked all but dry sometime during mid-spring, with flows returning mid-autumn when fishing picks up again.

Deschutes River, Upper
(Little Lava Lake to Wickiup Reservoir)

The diminutive Upper Deschutes River offers two distinct reaches, both of which are fairly popular with fly anglers. The first section flows between Little Lava Lake (the river's source) and Crane Prairie Reservoir. For the most part, small rainbow and brook trout inhabit this small stream, which meanders through lush meadows surrounded by lodgepole and ponderosa pines. Some big trout, however, thrive in the deep, marshy reach just below Little Lava Lake, a section which is best fished by float tube. Century Drive and several spur roads provide access to most of the river.

Below Crane Prairie Reservoir, the Deschutes gathers a bit more substance for about two and one half miles, and offers fair fishing for wild brook trout, rainbows and small brown trout. Some large fish are taken

each season from this scenic stretch of meandering meadow water between Crane Prairie and Wickiup reservoirs.

Wickiup's large brown trout spawn in this stream and the juvenile fish are largely reared here. Hence the river is closed during all but the summer months in an effort to protect spawning fish that have run up from the reservoir. During summer, however, this is fine dry-fly water, even though the average fish is fairly small. Access is from South Century Drive (Forest Primary Route 42). The Deschutes National Forest Map shows all the access points.

Upper Deschutes River
(Wickiup Dam to Bend)

Below Wickiup Dam, the Deschutes begins to form a substantial presence, picking up the flows of the Fall River and other tributaries as it swings northward. For most of its length, this part of the Deschutes meanders through broad meadows with much of the river on private property. The river's character changes entirely when it reaches Lava Butte, just a few miles south of Bend. Here the river picks up speed as it rushes through porous lava fields and over dangerous falls: Benham and Dillon falls have killed careless and unlucky boaters.

Various reaches of this portion of the Deschutes offer good fishing for rainbows and browns. Average fish are small, but large predatory brown trout inhabit the entire river from Wickiup Dam all the way to Lake Billy Chinook.

The first eight miles of meandering river below Wickiup Dam flows through public property down to Pringle Falls. If you float this section, heed the warning signs and exit the river above Pringle Falls: They are un-boatable and have been the scene of tragic mishaps in years past. Below Pringle Falls, the river winds its way through a mix of public and private property for some 16 miles down to Big River Campground. Boaters can put-in below the falls and float this entire section. Another nine-mile drift from Big River takes you to Bessen Campground near Spring River. The river below Spring River is boatable as far down as Benham Falls, but be sure you know when and where to exit the river above these very dangerous falls.

Bank access is good for most of the Deschutes between Wickiup and Bend, with the extensive private property in the Sunriver area offering a notable exception. The most direct access to the Wickiup Dam/Pringle Falls area is from Hwy. 97 south of Bend. You can follow South Century Drive (FR42) down from Sunriver or stay southbound on Hwy. 97 until you reach Wickiup Junction (Forest Primary Route 43) just north of LaPine. FR43 crosses the river near Pringle Falls and spur roads lead up- and downstream from there. Numerous campgrounds are found on the river and, of course, at all the nearby lakes.

On Hwy. 97, five miles north of Wickiup Junction, another main spur road leads west a few miles to LaPine State Recreation Area, which includes several miles of river. Watch for the signed turn-off about eight miles south of Sunriver.

The stretch of the Deschutes from Spring River to Bend, including the reach flowing through the lava fields of Lava Butte, is best accessed via Century Drive out of Bend. This is the road that leads to the ever-popular Mt. Bachelor Ski Area. Follow Century Drive west out of Bend for about seven miles and then turn south on Forest Route 41. Your Deschutes National Forest Map will guide you from there.

Little Deschutes River

This lengthy, meandering tributary of the Upper Deschutes River offers fair fishing for wild brown and rainbow trout. Only a dozen or so of the river's 90 miles flow through public lands, the rest being entirely within the confines of private property. Access is available only at a few bridge crossings and county road right-of-ways or by asking permission, which is always the best bet.

Anglers willing to knock on a few doors for permission may find some surprisingly good fishing: The Little Deschutes is home to some big, streamer-chasing browns. Obtain a copy of the Deschutes National Forest Map and begin the explorations.

Fall River

An attractive little spring creek that meanders its way through lodgepole and ponderosa stands southwest of Bend, the Fall River has in recent years become a favorite off-season destination for anglers in Central Oregon. The river was opened to winter catch-and-release fishing a few seasons back, giving fly fishers a chance to cast small nymphs and tiny dries to average-sized rainbows, brook trout and even a few brown trout.

During summer, the crowds gather but fishing remains productive because the ODFW stocks the stream on a regular basis (a two-fish limit is allowed). The fish run small, with legal-sized (10- to 12-inch) trout the norm. An occasional lunker brown or large carry-over rainbow can make things exciting, but with good trout cover at a premium above the falls, these are rare individuals.

The river is small and shallow and its waters gin clear, so careful approach and presentation will reap rewards, even on small trout, which quickly become wary of intrusion in this aquarium-like environment. Good hatches of midges and *Baetis* mayflies, along with localized hatches of PMDs and a few other mayflies, provide surface action; anglers adept at fishing tiny nymphs catch their share of the trout as well. Small and medium-sized streamers sometimes provide more action than anything else for those adept at swinging them through the feeding lanes with an erratic, dart-and-drift action. Summer fishing, especially during week days, is often quite productive as surface action is fairly reliable during mid-morning and evening, at least on most reaches of the river.

While the Fall River is among the prettiest spring creeks in the state, and attracts quite a lot of attention from fly anglers, don't expect a big-fish factory. This stream has little in common with classic Western spring creeks such as Hat Creek, the Henry's Fork and Silver Creek. First it lacks

Fall River.

JIM SCHOLLMEYER PHOTO

Fall River.   FRANK AMATO PHOTO

depth and cover; more importantly, its waters are comparatively infertile. Some big brown trout are found below the falls, some residents, others are migrants from the Deschutes. But above the falls, small trout are the rule and they exist in numbers only because of frequent stockings.

The Fall is easy to access. Follow Hwy. 97 south out of Bend some 12 miles to the Sunriver Exit. Turn west and follow the road past Sunriver and around a single S-curve. Immediately after coming out of the curves, turn left on South Century Drive (Route 42). Follow this road south, then west, crossing the Upper Deschutes River, and continue westerly until you see signs announcing Fall River. The area around the hatchery is popular, as is the water near the campground upstream near the springs.

To find a little more privacy, try any of several small spur roads and turn-outs that access the river from FR42 between the hatchery and the springs (about four miles of river). Or try the lower river, below the hatchery or even in the last mile or so below Fall River Falls. The lower river (below the hatchery) flows through a lot of private property where you will likely have to knock on a door to gain access. Forest Spur 4360 offers the best access to the river just above and below the falls. FR4360 turns south off FR42 about two miles west of Big River Bridge on the Deschutes. The road crosses the river about three quarters of a mile above the falls and trails lead up- and downstream from the bridge.

Crane Prairie Reservoir

Crane Prairie Reservoir, spanning 4,960 acres at full pool, ranks as one of the state's premier stillwater trout fisheries. The shallow, weedy waters of Crane Prairie promote rapid growth among the reservoir's rainbow trout, most of which are planted as fingerlings (a few wild rainbows, probably redbands, inhabit the reservoir as well).

Rainbows commonly span 10 to 16 inches, with lots of 18-inch fish available during good-water years. Rainbows to 10 pounds are taken every season, and fish in the four- to six-pound class are caught by fly anglers on a regular basis. Brook trout, though not caught as frequently, are planted in Crane periodically and these fish can reach five pounds or more. Between May and September—the prime growing season—trout

Crane Prairie Reservoir in the mist.

in Crane Prairie gain one to two inches each month, feasting on the reservoir's rich supply of scuds, damsels, dragons, mayfly nymphs, caddis, leeches and every other food item common to ideal stillwater trout habitat.

Despite its sprawling immensity, Crane Prairie averages only 11 feet deep and reaches a maximum depth of only 20 feet. Thus the entire lake bottom provides ample habitat for aquatic vegetation and in turn trout foods. When it's on, the early to midsummer damsel hatch is among the best in any Western reservoir, with massive numbers of emerging nymphs climbing out of the water on the abundant flooded snags and shoreline reeds. Similarly, the *Callibaetis* mayfly hatch can be heavy at times.

With such promise of large, hard-fighting rainbows feeding on damsels, mayflies and leeches, Crane Prairie attracts a crowd. District biologist Ted Fies classifies its use pattern as very heavy, a fact to which any Crane Prairie regular will attest.

Crane typically thaws in late March or April and is fishable by its opening date in late April assuming the roads are passable (the reservoir sits at an elevation of 4444 feet). Fishing holds up through most of the season, but a heavy, midsummer algae bloom can forestall the action for a short period of time, especially during long, hot summers. Late autumn fishing, for those willing to brave the sometimes frigid, unsettled weather, can be very productive.

In addition to the trout, Crane Prairie is home to a healthy population of largemouth bass, which were introduced illegally during the 1980s. Since then, the bass have thrived, with many reaching three to five pounds. At this point the trout seem to be holding their own, but fly anglers and biologists alike continually keep their fingers crossed that the bass won't eventually out-compete the trout. Serious bass anglers now flock to Crane Prairie

and so long as the bass are present, fly anglers might as well get in on the action. During late mid- to late summer, look for bass in heavy reed stands and shallow log-jam areas. Popper fishing can draw explosive strikes.

Much of the fishing pressure on Crane Prairie is concentrated around several popular and productive areas: The Deschutes Channel, Cultus River Channel, Quinn River Channel, Rocky Point and Rock Creek. Early season tends to find the trout scattered and often foraging in small schools. As summer weather begins to warm the water temperatures, the trout start to congregate in the old river channels and in a handful of deep holes. Cooler temperatures of autumn prompt the trout to disperse again, but their options are limited by the reservoir's drawdown, which peaks during September and October.

Crane Prairie is fairly good float-tube water assuming that you launch near your fishing destination in order to avoid excessively long paddles. A boat—even a small skiff—is a better option because you can move around the lake more easily, fishing one area for a while and then moving on if you don't find fish. Many anglers travel to favorite areas by boat and then launch float tubes when they get there.

About 45 miles southeast of Bend, Crane Prairie is flanked on the west by Century Drive, which also accesses other area lakes such as Hosmer, Sparks, Cultus and Wickiup Reservoir. From Bend, you can take the scenic route, going west and then south on Century Drive (Cascade Lakes Highway) past Mt. Bachelor and past Hosmer Lake, or you can take the quick route by following Hwy. 97 south to the Sunriver Exit or to the Fall River Road, both of which lead to the reservoir. Anglers coming from Eugene can take the Davis Lake cutoff from Hwy. 58, following signs to Route 46, which swings past Davis Lake and intersects Route 42, which reaches Crane Prairie. The Deschutes National Forest Map will keep you going in the right direction.

Crane Prairie Resort offers services and boat rentals, and several large campgrounds surround the reservoir: Cow Camp on the Deschutes Arm on the northeast shore, Crane Prairie Campground on the east shore near the resort, Rock Creek Campground and Quinn River Campgrounds off Route 46 (Cascade Lakes Highway) on the southwest shore and Cultus Campground.

Hosmer Lake

Hosmer Lake has long been a favorite destination for fly anglers because it boasts one of the West's few populations of landlocked Atlantic salmon. These hatchery-reared salmon average about 14 inches and reach 20 inches or a little more. Hosmer also supports a population of mostly hatchery brook trout, some of which reach several pounds. The big brook trout are difficult to hook and more difficult to land owing to their habit of running headlong into dense reed stands.

Pages 22-23: Hosmer Lake high in the Oregon Cascade Mountains feature landlocked Atlantic salmon.
Below: Landlocked Atlantic salmon take to the air in Hosmer Lake.

Bruce Bishoff with a rainbow from Crane Prairie Reservoir.

Landlocked Atlantic salmon.

Reaching a maximum depth of only 12 feet, Hosmer abounds in aquatic life, so much so that the salmon grow about an inch per month between late May and September. Caddis, *Callibaetis* mayflies, damsels, scuds, water beetles and boatmen, and Chironomids all play significant roles in the diet of Hosmer's salmon. Leech and streamer patterns can be effective as well, especially early and late in the season. Good dry-fly action occurs during strong *Callibaetis*, caddis and Chironomid hatches, but Hosmer's resident family of ospreys often prove an ample deterrent to fish that might otherwise rise freely.

Geographically, Hosmer is almost two separate lakes because a long, narrow channel connects the two main bodies of the lake. Big brook trout often cruise the channel and patient anglers might hook one here. Salmon, typically cruising in schools, frequent the channel as well. Also look for deeper water adjacent to reed stands, especially during the early summer damsel hatch. At 198 acres, Hosmer is great for canoes, float tubes and pontoon boats. Only electric motors are allowed. Catch-and-release regulations are in effect for the salmon and the entire lake is fly-fishing-only.

To reach Hosmer, follow the Cascade Lakes Highway (Century Drive) west out of Bend, continuing past Mt. Bachelor and past Sparks Lake, after which the highway swings to the south. Continue past Elk Lake and then look for the Hosmer Lake turnoff on the left (about 35 miles from Bend). There is ample camping space at Hosmer, except during holiday weekends and occasionally any other summer weekend, when the campgrounds can fill rapidly. Other campgrounds surround Elk Lake. Consult the Deschutes National Forest Map.

Angling pressure on Hosmer Lake is heavy, so if you are looking for solitude, fish early and late in the season or mid-week during the summer. Legally, Hosmer opens towards the end of April, but the lake generally doesn't thaw until May. October can be excellent. Another way to beat the crowds at Hosmer is to be on the water before first light in the morning.

Wickiup Reservoir

The largest of the lakes and reservoirs along the Cascade Lakes Highway at 10,334 acres (full pool), Wickiup Reservoir is home to some trophy-size brown trout, which reproduce naturally in the lake and whose numbers are also augmented by periodic stockings.

Without any special regulations in effect, most fly anglers leave Wickiup to the kokanee and coho trollers who work the lake all summer and fall. During autumn, however, Wickiup's brown trout begin to feed heavily in preparation for the late fall spawn. Between mid-September and late October, fly anglers can fish streamers off Gull Point near the Deschutes Channel and off the dam, as well as in the Deschutes Channel itself. Fifteen- to 18-inch brown trout are typical and quite a few fish will reach five or six pounds. A typical productive morning or evening during late fall might mean just a few fish hooked, but the chance for a brown better than 20 inches is strong incentive for the fly anglers who fish Wickiup on a regular basis.

The reservoir is loaded with Chironomids, along with lots of caddis and *Callibaetis* mayflies. During autumn when most of the fly-fishing action occurs, however, streamers and leech patterns are the rule. Float-tubers can put-in at Gull Point or at the dam—both places are adjacent to good areas for autumn fishing. Perhaps the easiest way to find fish is to troll with a fast-sinking line. During spring and early summer, the Davis Arm offers some of the best fly-rod action for rainbows and browns. Easy float-tube launches are located along, and just off, the highway.

Davis Lake

During the high-water years of the early 1980s, Davis Lake was one of the state's best trophy-trout waters, with 16- to 24-inch rainbows the norm. But the drought years that followed devastated this productive fishery as water seeped away through porous lava. Davis Lake began to

Davis Lake in early April.

rebound during the mid-1990s and by then most of the old crowd of Davis Lake regulars had turned to Crane Prairie for their trophy-trout chasing activities; newcomers to the sport hardly heard Davis Lake mentioned in local fly-angling circles except in the past tense.

As of this writing, Davis Lake has made a comeback thanks to wet winters during the mid-1990s. Davis Lake's fish grow rapidly on this shallow, fertile lake's abundant supply of chub minnows, scuds, damsels, snails, *Callibaetis*, caddis, dragonflies, leeches and other foods. The crowds of the pre-drought era have begun to re-assemble. Nonetheless, the new crop of rainbows in Davis Lake (Klamath Lake strain) typically span 16 to 18 inches with fish up to ten pounds available. These trout grow as much as two inches per month between May and October.

Like the other Central Oregon Cascade lakes, Davis is subject to a summer algae bloom, making spring, early summer and fall the best times to fish. One of the traditional attractions at Davis is the dragonfly hatch of late May through late June. This is one of the few lakes where

Davis Lake's Klamath-strain rainbow trout grow very quickly in this fertile Cascade lake.

Largemouth bass from Davis Lake.

you can watch dragonfly nymphs emerge from the water in large-enough quantities to qualify as an honest-to-God hatch. Years ago, Brent Snow introduced me to the Floating Dragonfly Nymph that proved so effective on Davis. Tied of spun deer hair, the Floating Dragon is fished on a sinking or sink-tip line. The line is allowed to sink, but the buoyant fly remains suspended above. A few quick strips of line and the fly appears to swim downward, toward the weed beds. The same fly can be fished on the surface during a heavy hatch: When the dragonfly nymphs are on the move en masse, the Floating Dragon sometimes draws explosive rises.

Davis also offers a good damsel emergence between May and mid-July and, on days when the wind stays down, a good *Callibaetis* hatch late spring through early fall. On occasion, caddis can hatch in dense-enough numbers to bring trout to the surface and evening midge hatches can be profuse. The mid-spring Chironomid hatch can be extremely dense at times, providing challenging dry-fly action. Leech patterns and streamers (e.g. Polar Chub, Gray Ghost, Mickey Finn, Dark Spruce, Zonker) are among the best flies for the early and late part of the season.

Davis Lake at early morning.

The Odell Creek arm of the lake fishes well early and late in the season, and the area around the lava flow on the northeast corner is a favorite location, especially during the damsel and dragonfly emergences. At nearly 4,000 acres when full, however, Davis offers lots of out-of-the-way nooks and crannies for anglers who want to find solitude.

Davis offers an additional fishery for largemouth bass, which were illegally introduced some time in the late 1980s or early 1990s. As of this writing (summer 1997), the bass population appears to have exploded, with the largest fish reaching about six pounds. They thrive in the backwater bays and coves as well as in parts of the main lake and will attack trout flies, streamers and popping bugs.

To reach Davis Lake from Bend, drive south on Hwy. 97 to the Sunriver turnoff (or to Vandeveer Road or Wickiup Junction). Follow any of these roads to South Century Drive and then up to Century Drive itself. Turn south and follow the highway past the west side of Wickiup Reservoir, past the lava flow and down to the well-marked turnoff to East Davis Campground. Another road turns off Century Drive and accesses West Davis Campground. From Eugene, follow Highway 58 over the pass and then take the Crescent-Davis Lake Cutoff Road, which meets Highway 58 a few miles southeast of Odell Lake.

Sparks Lake

Sparks Lake covers about 700 acres at full capacity, but does so with very little water, the average depth being about a foot or so when the extensive shallows are figured in. Nonetheless, when several high-water years stack up one after another, Sparks can produce brook trout to 16 inches or more. Sparks is a fly-only lake and is perfect for canoe enthusiasts. Early in the season, fish are scattered around the lake, but by midsummer they tend to congregate in the deeper areas (the deepest spot on the lake is about eight feet). The lake was created by a natural lava dam on the lake's south arm and when the water warms during the summer, fish tend to seek refuge in the cooler, deeper water near this dam.

Lava Lake
(Big Lava Lake and Little Lava Lake)

Located just a few miles south of Hosmer and Elk Lake on Cascade Lakes Highway southwest of Bend, Lava and Little Lava lakes offer decent fishing for rainbows and brook trout that will average a foot or less in length. Planted as fingerlings each year, both species attain about an inch per month during the growing season, so larger fish are available. Brook trout max out at about 16 inches, rainbows at about 20 inches.

Little Lava Lake, which lies immediately to the southeast of Lava Lake, is the source of the famed Deschutes River. Little Lava covers 138 acres and Lava Lake spans 340 acres. Both reach depths of more than 20 feet. Lava Lake is the more heavily fished of the two as it is adjacent to the highway. Both lakes have campgrounds and boat ramps.

Elk Lake

At 405 acres, Elk Lake is a fairly popular brook trout and kokanee lake on the Cascade Lakes Highway southeast of Bend. Elk Lake sits immediately west of Hosmer Lake. Brook trout average less than a foot in length with an occasional specimen reaching 18 inches.

Cultus Lake and Little Cultus Lake

Cultus Lake (792 acres) and Little Cultus Lake (175 acres) are located off the Cascade Lakes Highway a few miles northwest of, and across the highway from, Crane Prairie Reservoir. The big lake offers a few wild redband rainbows and legal-size hatchery rainbows along with lake trout (mackinaw) and native whitefish. Little Cultus, which lies south of Cultus Lake around the opposite side of Cultus Mountain, features planted brook trout and a few wild rainbows.

The hatchery rainbows planted in Cultus Lake often survive the winters well enough to provide opportunity for hold-overs that reach 14 or more inches. Lake trout average 18 to 20 inches and are rarely taken by fly anglers because of the depths at which they live during the summer (Cultus Lake averages 80 feet deep and reaches a maximum depth of 211 feet). However, if you can reach the lake soon after ice-out, you may find mackinaw foraging in the near-shore shallows where they can be taken on streamers. To reach Cultus Lake, follow Cascade Lakes Highway from Bend to the Cultus Lake road about 10 miles south of Elk Lake (look for the sign announcing Cultus Lake Lodge).

During summer, Cultus Lake is a playground for water skiers, recreational boaters and swimmers, so autumn offers the best and quietest time to try for the larger rainbows, which generally feed along the near-shore shallows.

Little Cultus Lake averages 10 to 25 feet deep with a maximum depth of 60 feet (in a deep hole near the west end). Its brook trout typically run eight to 10 inches, although fish to 15 inches are not uncommon. Little Cultus is comparatively lightly fished, which makes it a nice alternative when the better-known lakes get too crowded. All things considered, Little Cultus is probably the better lake for fly anglers because it offers better *Callibaetis*, Chironomid and caddis hatches and is better suited to float-tubing.

To reach Little Cultus, turn off on the road to Cultus Lake (FR4635), but turn left on FR4630 about a half-mile in. Stay to the right when the road forks and proceed less than a mile to Little Cultus. There is another approach to Little Cultus Lake from the west, but unless things have improved since I was last there, I wouldn't wish this road on my worst enemy. Campgrounds are located at both Little Cultus and Cultus lakes.

South Twin Lake

This heavily fished 99-acre lake lies just north of Wickiup Reservoir's Deschutes Arm. Despite its popularity, South Twin can provide good late-season fishing for 10- to 16-inch rainbows. Scuds and Chironomids predominate, but all the usual suspects are present in fair quantities, including *Callibaetis* mayflies and caddis. A leech pattern or small streamer (e.g. Woolly Bugger, Black Ghost, Marabou Muddler) fished on a sinking line will often provide constant action.

During summer, when a fierce breeze often howls across the big lakes (Crane Prairie, Wickiup and Davis), float-tubers become more numerous on South Twin as it is an excellent place to hide from the wind for a few hours.

Nearby North Twin Lake (130 acres) offers similar fishing for planted rainbows. Both lakes are easily accessed from Route 42 (South Century Drive). The entrance is about a mile east of the Deschutes River.

East Lake

Occupying a volcanic crater in the Paulina Mountains south of Bend, East Lake is a productive and popular fishery for rainbow trout, brown trout, kokanee, and landlocked Atlantic salmon. The lake is known for producing trophy browns, specimens to 20-plus inches are typical, though not necessarily common. The rainbows make up most of the catch and typically span 10 to 16 inches with fish to 20 inches available.

The Atlantic salmon are being stocked on an experimental basis and are showing up regularly in the catch. In years past, East Lake was popular for its autumn brook-trout fishing, but these fish are no longer stocked.

East Lake spans 1,044 acres at full pool and averages about 65 feet in depth with a maximum of 180 feet. The shoreline shallows provide the best fishing and float-tubers or boat anglers can fish over good *Callibaetis*, Chironomid and caddis hatches. The mayfly hatch lasts all summer and provides reliable surface activity almost every day. The shoreline region along both Hot Springs and East Lake Campground produces lots of fish. The east and west shorelines, along with the area around the cliffs on the north shore can all be very productive at times, especially during good hatches and during the early and late part of the season.

During non-hatch periods, scud patterns are productive (scuds are the lake's number one food item), as are any number of streamers, leech patterns and attractor wet flies like Carey Specials. If big brown trout are your goal, then troll or strip large streamers using a fast-sinking line

East Lake offers fair to good fishing for good-sized browns.

during the day or a medium-rate sinking line or sink-tip line along the drop-offs during morning and evening.

East Lake offers three campgrounds and several boat launches. Supplies, lodging and boat rentals are available at East lake Resort on the east shore. Paulina-East Lake Road heads east from Hwy. 97 north of La Pine, about 20 miles south of Bend. To reach East Lake, follow the road past Paulina Lake heading east. The area is a national monument, so a nominal entry fee is required and is payable at a booth on the way in.

Paulina Lake

At 1,500 acres, Paulina Lake sits just west of East Lake in Newberry Crater in the Paulina Mountains south of bend. Paulina is stocked with rainbows, browns and kokanee. Rainbows run 10 to 16 inches; brown trout can exceed 20 inches, even 30 inches, but are generally few and far between, especially in the larger sizes. The state-record brown trout—a fish of just under 28 pounds—came from Paulina in 1993 and the lake also boasts the state-record kokanee.

This heavily fished lake, which sits at an elevation of 6,350 feet, averages 163 feet deep and reaches a maximum depth of 250 feet. Without extensive shallows and shoal areas, Paulina Lake plays second fiddle to East Lake among fly anglers. Nonetheless, anglers who concentrate on the near-shore shallows along the north and northeast shore and adjacent to the resort in the outlet bay can find good fishing at times especially during autumn. Paulina is rich in scuds, *Callibaetis* and other food organisms; imitations of these food items produce all season and streamer patterns are effective throughout the year as well.

Two drive-in campgrounds are available along with two boat-in/hike-in campgrounds on the north shore. Paulina Lake Resort offers lodging, a restaurant, boat rentals and other amenities. Follow Hwy. 97 south about 20 miles from Bend and then turn east on Paulina-East Lake Road, which climbs up Paulina Mountain about 12 miles to the lake. Paulina Creek, which roughly parallels Paulina-East Lake Road, offers fair fishing at times, especially if you venture to its unvisited reaches away from the roads. The area is a national monument, so a nominal entry fee is required at a booth on the way in.

Odell Lake

The main attraction at Odell Lake—a beautiful mountain lake in the high Cascades adjacent to Hwy. 58—are large lake trout (mackinaw) and abundant kokanee. Thus Odell Lake is primarily a playground for trollers. Mackinaw can be taken on a streamer here, but only if you are lucky enough to time your trip to coincide with ice-out, when the macs often cruise near-shore shallows. The better bet for this kind of fishing is nearby Crescent Lake. Odell Lake also offers a lightly fished population of nice rainbows, which respond eagerly to the lake's *Callibaetis* hatches during the summer. Fish the shallow shoreline areas for trout that run 10 to 20 inches.

Suttle Lake

Adjacent to Hwy. 20/126 just east of the Santiam Pass summit, Suttle Lake offers wild brown trout and kokanee along with native mountain whitefish. Brown trout—the main attraction for fly anglers—average a healthy 16 inches, but are not particularly plentiful. Nonetheless, anglers who fish early and late in the season (before and after the heavy summer algae bloom sets in) might connect with a brown trout in the 20-inch-plus range.

Suttle Lake is heavily fished owing to its proximity to the highway and to its kokanee population, but those willing to brave cold water during late April and cold weather during October won't have much company. At 253 acres, Suttle Lake is reasonable for float-tubers and boaters alike. The lake reaches a maximum depth of 75 feet with an average depth of 44 feet. Sinking lines and large flies are the rule—try big leech patterns, crayfish patterns and streamers that imitate juvenile whitefish and kokanee.

Hood River

The Hood River draws its headwaters directly from the glaciers on Mt. Hood and thus its waters flow off-color with glacial particulate matter during the summer. Nonetheless, the river offers fair fly angling for summer and winter steelhead. The summer fish begin arriving in the river during late spring and continue into the fall. The best fly fishing occurs from early to mid-fall when air temperatures on Mt. Hood dip below freezing, locking up the glacial flow and allowing the river to run clear. Winter-run fish arrive between December and April.

Most steelhead are taken within the lower 10 miles of the system, but each fork of the river—the West Fork, Middle Fork and the East Fork—offers steelhead in fishable numbers during good years. Pay close attention to the fishing regulations, however, as they seem to be in constant flux for this watershed. As of this writing, most of the system is open for steelhead with exceptions being Pinnacle Creek and Lake Branch (Middle Fork), which are closed to all fishing.

The forks of the Hood River converge near the community of Dee, some 12 miles south by southwest of the town of Hood River. To reach Dee, follow Hwy. 35 south out of Hood River and follow the signs.

Early summer on East Lake signals the beginning of the *Callibaetis* mayfly hatch.

SOUTHEAST ZONE

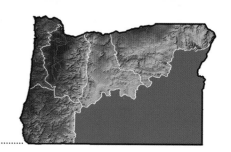

Geographically speaking, the Southeast Zone covers a huge chunk of the state and is far larger than any other zone. However, since a large portion of this zone receives precious little rainfall, it is also the driest zone in the state. Oregon's largest and least populated counties—Harney, Malheur and Lake—are included in the Southeast Zone, all of them dominated by semi-arid conditions. Despite the harsh climate, southeastern Oregon offers much of interest to the fly angler.

Included in this zone is the Klamath Basin: Klamath Lake, with its huge rainbows, is Oregon's largest lake; the Williamson, Klamath, Wood and Sprague rivers are well known among fly anglers. East, across the hills from the Klamath Basin, begins Oregon's desert country. From the streams and reservoirs near Lakeview east to the Steens Mountain region and north to the Powder River country, fly anglers will find ample good fishing with numerous opportunities to pursue large trout.

Regional favorites include ever-popular Mann Lake, with its Lahontan cutthroat fishery, and wind-lashed Chickahominy Reservoir, which sits beside the main east-west artery through this country, Highway 20. Desert streams like the Blitzen, Malheur, Owyhee and others offer solitude and good fishing for those willing to work a little.

In fact, many tiny desert streams that drain the region's highest mountain ranges, offer fair fishing for native redband trout and redband/cutthroat hybrids. The best of these streams are remote and tiny, just a few feet wide and a foot or two deep in the pools. Because of their fragility, I have chosen not to include them by name and I trust you will understand this decision. Besides, fly anglers willing to go to the extremes of reaching these waters tend to be the type who don't mind doing a little homework or a little legwork

Meanwhile, the region is resplendent in its varied geology and spectacular vistas. Among the must-see sights are Abert Rim and the Steens Mountains, awesome fault-block escarpments whose dimensions defy description; the Alvord Desert, whose sand and alkaline expanse shimmers in illusionary watery dances during the summer; the Owyhee Canyon and Succor Creek, landscapes that would seem more fitting in the deserts of Arizona.

As you explore the wide vistas of southeast Oregon, fly rod in hand, keep an eye peeled for the wonderment of the Great Basin landscapes, the abundant wildlife that is so well adapted to this country, and the rich sense of history: petroglyphs on the rocks, obsidian shards left from centuries of native craftsmanship, stone rings marking the sites of temporary villages in which resided nomadic bands of Paiutes, Klamath and Modoc peoples. But keep that fly rod at the ready because some of Oregon's best trout fisheries are found in the expanses of southeastern and south-central Oregon.

Lastly, for those unfamiliar with traveling the remote parts of southeastern Oregon, I'll offer some advice. Always carry the following: Lots of water, extra fuel for the vehicle, *at least* one spare tire (and make sure your jack assembly is in good working order), jumper cables, tire chains or cables, shovel, extra food, and warm clothes. Preparedness becomes increasingly important as you venture further away from civilization, especially to places like Spaulding and Sid's reservoirs, Deep Creek, or the remote waters of the Alvord country.

Lahontan cutthroat commonly span 18 to 22 inches in Mann Lake.

Mann Lake offers good fishing for Lahontan cutthroat in a remarkable setting.

Mann Lake

Mann Lake, located at the eastern foot of the rugged Steens Mountains, is Oregon's premier fishery for Mann Lake cutthroat, an Oregon hatchery version of Lahontan cutthroat trout. Originally from Lake Lahontan in Nevada, these cutthroat are adapted to the highly alkaline waters of natural lakes in the Great Basin.

ODFW biologists capture Mann Lake fish in order to harvest eggs, which are then transported to a hatchery where the fish are born and raised to fingerlings before being planted in Mann Lake and certain other waters. Natural reproduction has never been documented in Mann Lake; the fishery is maintained by stocking every other year and by harvest restrictions.

Stocked as yearlings, these fish grow rapidly in Mann Lake's shallow, fertile broth. By fall, yearling cutthroat run 10 to 12 inches. The average fish from Mann Lake exceeds 14 inches and 18- to 20-inch fish are common. Maximum size is about 24 inches.

Historically, Mann Lake covers about 250 acres. The high-water years of the early 1980s, when Malheur and Harney counties were inundated with disastrous flood waters, filled Mann Lake to unheard-of levels. The cutthroat thrived as the lake doubled in size. More-or-less back to normal now, Mann Lake averages only eight feet deep and reaches a maximum depth of about 15 feet. Tremendous weed growth provides abundant habitat for a rich supply of scuds, damsels, snails, Chironomids, water beetles, leeches and other aquatic trout foods. The lake freezes most winters, retaining an ice cover from December until late February.

Anglers converge on the lake as early as March and the entire spring is a busy time these days. During June, warm water and dense weed growth slows the fishing until fall, when cool weather rejuvenates the lake. Mid-autumn can offer exceptional fishing for bright cutthroat, but the weather can turn bitter cold. April and May are the most popular months on the lake. Springtime hatches of large Chironomids offer mid-morning dry-fly fishing at times and the damsel hatch typically starts during mid- to late May.

Mann Lake is an excellent float-tube lake, but wading anglers often predominate: The cutthroat frequent the shallows and most of the shoreline is easy to wade. Floating, intermediate and sink-tip lines are most useful. During the early morning and evening hours—when the wind stays down—you can sight-fish to cruising cutts in less than a foot of water.

Mann Lake anglers must be prepared to fend for themselves in a remote environment that can turn nasty with little warning. The Steens Mountains, which provide a spectacular backdrop against the lake, help create howling winds that can whip the lake into a white-capped frenzy. One year, during April, I was surprised to see a big, dark object zooming overhead about 100 feet above the lake. As it blew rapidly past the end of the lake, I was able to identify the object as a two-man tent; I'm reasonably certain the two men were not inside, but given the ferocity of that wind, I can't be sure.

Similarly, on many occasions I've watched as a wall of white descended down the slope or approached from the south, enveloping everything in its path in a blinding blizzard of snow. Frequently a bright morning will eventually yield to a howling wind, making the lake virtually unfishable until evening. The lake and its surroundings offer no shelter from the weather, so bring your own in the form of a truck, camper, RV or sturdy tent. The nearest juniper is too far away come nasty weather and the nearest civilization outside of a few ranches is the tiny town of Fields about 50 miles to the south.

Mann Lake offers few amenities. A few years ago, the BLM installed pit toilets. The lake has a couple of gravel boat ramps. There is no drinking water, no formal campground and no firewood. Mann Lake's remoteness, however, coupled with the stunning scenery and big cutthroats, makes it a favorite destination for many fly anglers.

To reach Mann Lake, follow Highway 78 south of Burns, past the town of Crane and the village of New Princeton. Eventually, the highway leads through a winding mountain pass. As you reach the far (south) end of the pass, watch for a gravel turnoff on the right with a sign pointing the way to Fields. This is the Fields-Denio Road. The wide gravel highway leads some 25 miles to Mann Lake. Along the way, you will pass 10 Cent, 15 Cent and Juniper lakes on the right, but don't mistake these for Mann (all three can be dry or nearly dry). After passing Juniper Lake, you will flank a large, dry lake called Tudor Lake (home to lots of water and huge rainbows during the early 1980s) on your left. Continue past Tudor Lake, over a slight rise and down the slope to Mann Lake, which will be visible on your right. On a typical weekend, all the vehicles will assure you that you've found Mann Lake.

Nice side trips include the run down to Alvord Hot Springs north of Fields and the town of Fields itself, where one small restaurant serves up a mean milkshake. Slot machines are but a few miles to the south at the border town of Denio.

Chickahominy Reservoir

Chickahominy Reservoir, located about 100 miles east of Bend along Highway 20, is one of eastern Oregon's best stillwater fisheries, at least during periods of average or better water tables. This large desert reservoir offers rainbow trout to 20 inches, sometimes larger, whose girth almost rivals their length. These are all planted trout, but they grow quickly in Chickahominy's shallow, fertile waters. Three-inch fingerlings planted in the spring will average 10 to 12 inches by fall.

Chickahominy anglers, however, must be tolerant: tolerant of high winds and cold weather; tolerant of the crowd of RVs parked on the east bank, these belonging to the horde of trollers, worm-drowners and Powerbaiters that have inhabited the reservoir for as long as I can remember. Their presence never seems to affect the fishing too much—despite the fact that each spring I try to get my licks in early for fear that the meat-hunters will divest the reservoir of its trout before the season is half over. This never seems to happen, at least not during good water years.

Chickahominy Reservoir is one of southeast Oregon's most popular fisheries

The meat-hunters are just part of the package so Chick's fly anglers accept them (or maybe its the other way around). As for fly-casters, they are generally few in number. The busiest of spring weekends might find three or four dozen fly anglers spread out over this sprawling 800-acre desert reservoir. Go mid-week and you might have a cove or two all to yourself.

Fishing begins at ice-out, typically sometime in February. Early on, look for fish cruising the shoreline shallows, often in a foot or two of water. For the first two or three weeks you can stalk these 14- to 24-inch bruisers in the "fingers" (narrow bays) on the reservoir's west side. Soon after, the trout milling about in the upstream extent of these fingers will be more interested in spawning than in eating, although successful reproduction has never been documented.

Chickahominy's rainbows feed heavily on all sorts of aquatic organisms, including midge larvae and pupae, snails, leeches, water beetles, scuds, Callibaetis nymphs and damsel nymphs. The midge hatch begins soon after ice-out and provides reliable surface activity as early as March. By April, tremendous evening hatches of bloodworm midges prompt frenzied action at dusk.

Meanwhile any number of small nymphs will take trout during the day. Top producers include Zug Bugs, Pheasant Tails, Prince Nymphs, Hare's Ears and scuds, all on sizes 10-14. The same patterns tied with a small brass bead at the head are effective also. Woolly Buggers produce early, but smaller, dark nymphs are the ticket during most of the spring and early summer.

Given the shallow, weedy water, I generally opt for a floating line and long leader. Early in the spring, before the weed growth has really started, a sinking or sink-tip line, rigged with Chironomid pupae, snail patterns or small nymphs often produces when other methods fail.

The first sparse hatches of Callibaetis mayflies (speckle-winged duns) and damsels occur during May. The Callibaetis hatch needn't be heavy to interest a few trout. Look for wind-drift lanes and leeward shorelines where emerging duns concentrate on breezy afternoons.

Chickahominy is characterized by extensive shallows, ample weed growth and a bottom ranging from sticky ooze to sandy gravel to firm mud. The reservoir is also renowned for its wind, hence our old code-name, "Hurricane Lake." A typical day begins with the calm of early morning, but by late morning or noon, the breeze begins to whip the surface until the entire lake is covered with rolling whitecaps. A stiff, relentless wind generally blows through late afternoon or early evening, sometimes well into the night. The occasional still day is a treat to be cherished.

Nothing deflects the wind. It simply howls across miles of open sage plains and sweeps across the reservoir, beating the water to a turbid, surging froth. More than the stark, barren setting and long drive, I think the unforgiving wind keeps folks away from Chickahominy.

Given a few years of good water supply, Chickahominy can grow rainbows to trophy sizes.

Yellowjacket Lake

At only 20 acres, Yellowjacket Lake is a small reservoir located north of Burns in the Malheur National Forest. Planted rainbows go eight to 18 inches in the shallow, fertile reservoir and an occasional wild redband drifts in from the creek above. This good float-tube lake features a USFS campground and a gravel boat ramp. Yellowjacket is accessed by Forest Road 47 out of Hines (Burns). Follow FR47 north out of Hines until you reach the signed turnoff to Yellowjacket (FR37). Snow blocks access during spring, so call ahead to the ODFW office in Hines to see if the road is passable. As with most reservoirs in southeast Oregon, Yellowjacket is best during spring and fall. However, June and July fishing can be very productive during high-water years.

Delintment Lake

Located in the Ochoco National Forest some 35 miles northwest of Burns, 52-acre Delintment Lake offers fair to good fishing for average-sized rainbows, with an occasional fish to 18 inches. A good float-tube lake early in the season, Delintment winterkills most years. After a mild winter, hold-over trout can reach decent sizes. To reach this heavily fished lake, follow the signed road (FR47) north out of Hines. Forest Road 47 will meet FR41, which takes you all the way to the lake. Snowpack limits access during spring, so be sure to check ahead by calling the ODFW office in Hines.

Malheur River System

The Malheur River is a complex and important river system draining much of the southeastern Oregon high desert. Its forks emanate from the Blue Mountains northeast of Burns. The river offers three forks: The South Fork, North Fork and the mainstem, simply called the Malheur.

Rod Robinson fishes the Malheur River in late winter.

The rest of us deal with it. We fish the coves, where the water often remains a little more clear than the lake proper and we seek the windward shorelines, where a narrow band of calm water lies protected under the slope of the shoreline rise. On slow days, we might wind-drift by launching tubes or boats at one end of the reservoir and drifting to the far end, dragging flies behind or casting off to the sides.

A boat or float tube often comes in handy, but wading the shoreline generally produces as well or better than floating. In short, Chickahominy is a love-it, hate-it kind of a deal: Those willing to forgive the windy, cold, hostile, barren expanse and the crowd of meat-hunters, love those big, fat, leaping rainbows.

Chickahominy lies on the north side of Hwy. 20 about 100 miles east of Bend and about 35 miles west of Burns. Meager supplies are sometimes available a few miles east of Chickahominy at the little wide spot of Riley, whose store/gas station is open only when the current owners have not yet lost their shirts on the deal, boarded up and posted "For Sale" signs in the windows.

Bring your own water and shelter; firewood if desired. A rough dirt road (mud during early spring and wet weather) accesses the west shoreline. Use extreme caution on this road early in the year as each season several people bury their vehicles (cars and 4X4s alike) up to the axles on this gooey road. This rutted-out track angles away to the left from the main access road just after you turn off the highway. The better road leads across the dam to the so-called campground, where the RV crowd assembles. Beyond this fee campground, the road continues along the east shoreline, where more good fly-water awaits. Most fly anglers rough it by setting up camp along the meandering western shoreline or on the northeast shore. Expect cold nights at least through April and again in the fall.

FRANK AMATO PHOTO

The Malheur River can produce rainbows up to 20 inches during years of good water supply.

The South Fork, which suffers from poor water quality and severe irrigation drawdown, occasionally offers fair fishing for wild redbands, but this small desert stream flows almost entirely through private property. A knock on a rancher's door can get you permission to explore this diminutive fork of the Malheur, which joins the mainstem at Riverside, east of Warm Springs Reservoir. More common in the South Fork are small-mouth bass, especially near the mouth. Most of the bass are rather small.

Warm Springs Reservoir, in fact, creates one of the Malheur's most productive reaches in the form of a tailwater fishery from Riverside to Juntura. This is remote and rugged canyon country with no drive-in access between the crossing at Riverside and the little town of Juntura. Some primitive dirt roads approach the canyon's rim, but you must walk down to the river, often over some difficult terrain. This dozen-odd-mile reach from Riverside to Juntura is floatable most years, but be wary of the countless jagged boulders.

In this section, planted rainbows and some wild Redband trout reach 20 inches, although 12- to 16-inch fish are more typical and their abundance depends a great deal on water supply. Given two or three consecutive high-water years, trout populations remain healthy, but the river runs muddy until fall. Sometimes early to mid-spring offers decent fishing during high-water years. During dry years, the river may flow reasonably clear by mid- to late spring, but sometimes the entire fishery is devastated by a summer flush of warm water from Warm Springs Reservoir. All things considered, mid- to late fall usually offers the best fishing because the water runs clear. Before venturing to this remote area, check with ODFW on the status of the fishery.

Caddis hatches can be dense during spring and early summer; fishable but not so heavy during fall. *Baetis* (blue-winged olive) mayflies hatch from late winter through mid-spring and again during the fall. Throughout early summer and again during fall, hopper fishing can be excellent.

Below Juntura, Hwy. 20 follows the Malheur, first through a picturesque canyon and then out onto the agricultural lands near Vale. The canyon stretch can provide decent fishing at times, but rarely does it compare to the waters between Riverside and Juntura.

Upstream from Warm Springs Reservoir, the Malheur flows across a 15-mile-long expanse of desert below the little town of Drewsey. Redbands and smallmouth bass, along with rough fish, inhabit this stretch and populations of all these fish were severely depleted during a major drought from the late 1980s through the early 1990s. Access here is limited: All the water from Drewsey to about two miles south of Hwy. 20 is private ranch property. Below this, the Malheur flows through a mixture of state and BLM property until it reaches Warm Springs Reservoir, the upper arm of which is surrounded by Bureau of Reclamation lands. Road access is by 4-wheel-drive primitive roads leading in off the Warm Springs Reservoir Road to the west and the Chimney Creek Road on the east, both of which turn south off Hwy. 20. The

Dave Hughes on the Malheur River.

Malheur River rainbow.

Warm Springs Reservoir Road is the better choice. Check the BLM Burns District maps (North Half) before venturing into this country and be extremely wary of wet road surfaces.

Above Drewsey, the river flows entirely through private property, but many of the parcels are smaller, with houses aplenty where one can seek permission to fish for the river's wild redbands. Fishing can be good, especially during hopper season and when several high-water years occur in succession. The Drewsey-Van Road follows the north side of the river and Drewsey Market Road follows more closely along the south bank. The roads connect upstream and form a long loop through Drewsey Valley and Kimball Flat.

The Malheur's attractive headwaters gather from the Logan Valley on the south slopes of the Strawberry Mountains southeast of John Day. Fairly remote in these upper reaches, the river offers good fishing for wild Redband rainbows that occasionally reach 18 to 20 inches. Bull trout, now fully protected, inhabit the entire upper watershed in small numbers.

The first 10 miles of river within the Malheur National Forest are designated as Wild & Scenic. Forest Primary Route 16 accesses the headwaters and a campground is located on Big Creek, a major tributary. South of FR16, Big Creek flows through private property. However, you can turn south on FR1647 about a mile east of the campground, drive three miles, and find the trailhead for the Malheur Scenic Trail.

A short distance further south, Forest Road 1651 crosses the river at Malheur Forde and from here anglers walk up- or downstream on good trails. On the west side of the river, at Dollar Basin, FR1651 arrives at FR1643, which follows the river (at a distance) to the Hog Flat area. The last two miles of the Wild & Scenic reach are located south of Skookum Canyon. Then the Malheur flows through two miles of private property before entering BLM land for three miles. The last few miles of the Wild & Scenic section and these three miles of BLM frontage, offer the least-visited water of the upper river because no roads approach closer than about a mile. Before venturing out, obtain copies of the Malheur National Forest Map and the BLM's Burns District Recreation Guide, North Half.

To reach the headwaters of the Malheur, follow Hwy. 395 north from Burns or south from John Day until you arrive at the little town of Seneca. From Seneca, turn east on Primary Route 16 and drive some 20 miles to Big Creek.

The fishing is pretty straightforward: Basic attractor-type dry flies work most of the time and large streamers (e.g. Woolly Buggers, Marabou Muddlers) can tempt the largest fish to leave the cover of deep pools and undercut banks. Grasshopper season probably offers the best dry-fly fishing and extends from July through September. Some stretches of the upper river offer good late spring/early summer hatches of large stoneflies, but the fishing depends a lot on the volume of snow-melt.

The North Fork Malheur flows into Beulah Reservoir and its upper reaches are also designated as a Wild & Scenic River. The North Fork offers wild redband rainbows that can reach 20 inches, although a 10-inch specimen would be more typical. Protected bull trout are present as well. The uppermost reaches of the North Fork are easily accessed off Forest Primary Route 13. Follow County Road 62 southeast out of Prairie City for about eight miles, then turn east at FR13, along Deardorff Creek, one of the John Day River's source streams. At Short Creek Guard Station, FR13 meets FR16, which arrives from Logan Valley.

About two miles south of Short Creek Guard Station on FR16, a spur road (FR1675) heads southeast down to North Fork Malheur Campground. Below the campground, a good trail leads south along the river and continues for 10 miles, all the way to the national forest boundary. National forest spur roads follow the river from above, but access to the canyon below Crane Creek Camp is difficult. Pick your spot wisely with the help of a USGS topo map, however, and you can access remote sections of the river with a little walking. Between the Malheur National Forest boundary and Beulah Reservoir, the river flows mostly through private property, although it crosses several BLM parcels.

Big rainbows are taken regularly in the tailwater of Agency Valley Dam on Beulah Reservoir. Large nymphs and streamers will do the trick assuming you can fish around the bait-anglers and plunkers. Access is through the gatekeeper's drive and this tailwater is on private property. Rarely do the worm-dunkers ask permission, but it is a good policy (and the right thing to do) for fly anglers to stop in and ask for permission. Tailwater trout span 14 to 20-plus inches. Access is the same as for Beulah Reservoir (see heading): turn north on a well-marked road off Hwy. 20 at the west edge of Juntura and drive 17 miles up to the dam.

Beulah Reservoir

Water, or lack thereof, is paramount to Beulah's potential as a fishery. Typically this high-desert reservoir is drawn down heavily during summer to feed the needs of area agriculture. Just keeping water in the reservoir at all has been problematic over the past decade or so and each time Beulah has gone dry, Oregon Department of Fish & Wildlife has been forced to start from scratch with the fishery. However, during periods of good water supply, Beulah's chunky rainbows span 12 to 20-plus inches, making it one of the best stillwater destinations in southeastern Oregon.

Beulah Reservoir's chunky rainbows grow fast during good water years.

Beulah Reservoir during late spring.

Beulah Reservoir is located in the hills north of Juntura, Oregon, about halfway between Burns and Vale. At the west edge of Juntura, turn north off Hwy. 20 onto Beulah Road (signs announce Beulah Reservoir and Chukar Park). Follow the gravel road along the North Fork Malheur up to the reservoir. Once you arrive, the main road continues along the east shoreline while a second road crosses the dam and accesses a short length of the west bank.

At or near full pool, Beulah is a big reservoir. The east shoreline offers lots of good shallow float-tube water where weed beds grow and trout cruise morning and evening. During the day, move just a little farther off shore and fish a sinking line.

While Beulah may not be quite as rich as other eastern Oregon shallow-water reservoirs, like Chickahominy and Malheur, it nonetheless produces tremendous quantities of aquatic trout foods, especially when three or four consecutive wet years allow for year-round water supply. Beulah's trout grow rapidly on a diet rich in scuds, snails, water beetles, Chironomids, leeches, damsels and other critters.

A few redband trout and bull trout wander into Beulah from the North Fork Malheur, but the fishery centers primarily on planted rainbows. The fish grow fast, but during good years, bait fishermen take lots of trout out of Beulah. Essentially, fishing productivity depends a lot on relative abundance of these rainbows.

During morning and evening, at times when fish populations are high, expect good shoreline fishing. When fish populations are down, try float-tube trolling or simply moving around quite a bit until you start finding fish—then fish that area thoroughly. The fishing begins during mid-spring (call ODFW to check on ice-out and road conditions; 541/573-6582) and will hold up until high water temperatures and low lake levels promote heavy algae blooms during summer. By fall, trout populations are reduced, but so to are water levels and the number of meat-hunters. In my estimation, late September through mid-October is the prime time at Beulah during years of good water supply.

Because Beulah is subject to year-to-year changes in the productivity of its fishery, anglers should call ODFW in Hines (Burns) for up-to-date reports before making the drive. If you are coming from any distance, you will want some back-up plans, which might include Mann Lake, Malheur Reservoir, Chickahominy or any of the numerous other destinations in southeastern Oregon.

Owyhee River

Not all that long ago, Oregon's Owyhee River trickled from Owyhee Dam, forming a little-known and productive tailwater fishery for large rainbow and brown trout. While the fishery remains productive, the "little known" part is a thing of the past, a victim of the population explosion in Boise and surrounding southwestern Idaho: The Owyhee lies within a one- to two-hour drive of Idaho's population center.

These days, fly anglers who fish the Owyhee in solitude do so in the spring and fall and on weekdays during the summer. Even a crowded day, however, cannot divest the Owyhee of its desert beauty. After spilling from Owyhee Dam, which backs up 40-mile-long Owyhee Reservoir, the river meanders through a deep canyon lined with massive rimrocks and towering rock escarpments which glow red in the desert sunrise.

Most fishing on the Owyhee occurs during the summer, when water levels are stable. Spring can be good when water levels are reasonable and autumn can be exceptional given the same stable water levels characteristic of summer.

Summer offers some good hatches, especially caddis hatches, but also *Callibaetis* and *Baetis* mayflies along with some stonefly activity. The Owyhee's hatches can be highly localized because the river's character varies quite a bit: slow, deep pools in one section, followed by shallow riffles followed by boulder-strewn pocket water and gliding runs. Terrestrial patterns can be highly productive during summer, especially in backeddies and along steep banks.

Given stable water levels, spring can offer good hatches of March browns and blue-winged olives along with midges and a few winter stoneflies. These hatches, too, are localized. If water levels are fishable during mid- to late-spring, look for good caddis hatches during warm weather. The same is true during the fall.

No minimum flow is allowed for the Owyhee's planted trout, but summer water levels usually remain fairly constant. Fall can be a different story, however, as the dam is usually corked until the following spring, resulting in severely reduced winter flows. Often, the river freezes during winter and the fish take refuge in the deeper pools. If the river remains ice-free, brave souls can dredge up a few trout during winter while sharing the canyon with chukar hunters until mid-January. The more prudent choice might be to leave the pool-bound trout to their task of surviving the winter and have at them again when flows return in the spring.

Oregon Department of Fish and Wildlife plants the Owyhee every second year with 3,000 yearling brown trout and annually with 40,000 rainbow fingerlings. Despite annual electroshock surveys, biologists have never documented natural reproduction of either species. District biologist Wayne Bowers did tell me of unconfirmed reports of redds, which might suggest spawning activity. These have not been documented by ODFW.

Both species can attain impressive sizes in the Owyhee's rich waters. Fourteen- to 20-inch trout are common and 5- to 6-pound trout are taken every year by both fly anglers and terminal-gear anglers.

Even during winter the Owyhee River can offer good fishing, including some dry-fly action.

KEN MORRISH

Blitzen River.

The campground at Snively Hot Springs is the lower limit for trout during the summer. Below Snively, the water slows markedly and gets too warm for trout. This leaves anglers with about 10 miles of river between the campground and Owyhee Dam, all of it paralleled by a paved road. Rough camping is available along the river in side-canyons.

Idaho anglers can reach the Owyhee via U.S. 95, which is the main north-south route along the western Idaho border. Follow the signs to the town of Nyssa and then to the tiny village of Owyhee where signs will lead to Owyhee State Park; or cross the Snake River near Marsing or Homedale and follow State Route 19 (201 in Oregon) across the border and north to Owyhee. From the north, anglers can follow Interstate 84 to Ontario and then head for Nyssa and Owyhee. From the west, turn south at the east end of Vale and follow a network of roads leading to the river (follow the Owyhee State Park signs). A phone call to the ODFW office in Ontario or to one of the Boise-area fly shops might be a good idea before you venture off to this productive little desert tailwater.

Blitzen River

The diminutive Blitzen River offers fair to good fishing for wild redband trout in a remote canyon setting on the west slope of the Steens Mountains. The Blitzen runs high and murky during spring and early summer, so fly anglers generally wait until July to fish this rugged river. A BLM campground (Page Springs) is located at the mouth of Blitzen Canyon southeast of the tiny town of Frenchglen. From Page Springs you

can hike up. Or you can access the stream from Steens Mountain Loop Road, which crosses the river at Blitzen Crossing. The easiest way to reach Blitzen Crossing is to pass through Frenchglen and then follow Hwy. 205 as it winds up the rim behind town and heads south towards Fields. The Loop Road turns east off the highway several miles before you reach Roaring Springs Ranch. Other primitive roads access the canyon at various points. Consult the BLM's Steens Mountains Recreational Area map.

Krumbo Reservoir

Krumbo Reservoir, located on the Malheur Wildlife Refuge north of Frenchglen, offers good early and late-season fishing for rainbows that average about 12 inches and reach 20-plus inches. Krumbo covers 150 acres and averages less than 20 feet deep.

Rich in trout foods, Krumbo's planted rainbows grow fast. Largemouth bass are present as well. Most of the pressure occurs during April and May; fly anglers often find better fishing during mid- to late fall. Overnight camping is not allowed.

To reach Krumbo, follow Hwy. 78 out of Burns and then turn right (south) on Hwy. 205 to Frenchglen. The signed turnoff to Krumbo Reservoir is about nine miles north of Frenchglen. The nearby Diamond Craters make for an interesting side trip.

Ana River

The Ana River is a small spring creek whose natal springs gush from the sandy bluffs just below Ana Reservoir. The stream glides southerly, meandering its way just a few miles before reaching Summer Lake Marsh. The reach between the reservoir and the refuge offers fair to good fishing for planted rainbow trout that occasionally reach 18 or 20 inches. Average fish span eight to 14 inches and they look like wild fish because they are planted as fingerlings.

Throughout most of this stretch, the Ana flows through a small but precipitous desert ravine, some of it choked with scrub brush. Most anglers simply walk the top of the bluff above the river and watch for rising trout below. Having spotted a riser or two, an angler can then choose a descent down the steep little canyon. In places, good trails follow along the river bank. The Ana is floatable by raft, pontoon boat or float tube, but the river is so small that

Ana River and alkali-covered banks.

FRANK AMATO PHOTO

walking may be the more prudent choice, especially if other anglers are about. I once stood in awe as a drift boat steered by, its oars each reaching one bank in the tight quarters of a narrow S-curve.

Most of the river is shallow, its bottom combining clean gravel patches with rich weed beds. In places, narrow channels, corners, overhangs and culverts provide deep-water habitat for the river's largest trout.

Blue-winged olive mayflies (*Baetis*) and midges (Chironomids) provide much of the surface activity and the hatches of both can be heavy and long-lasting affairs at times. Pale morning duns, Tricos and brown drakes hatch as well, but rarely in substantial or sustained bursts. Caddis activity is dominated by tiny "micro-caddis." During summer and fall, terrestrial insects abound. These include hoppers, ants, beetles and spiders.

Given the Ana's smooth, gliding surface, it's no wonder that dry-fly action fuels the anticipation. When surface action is not forthcoming, however, try small nymphs like Pheasant Tails and Cressbugs, or fish streamers in the deep pools and culvert holes.

To reach the Ana River, follow Hwy. 31 south of the town of Silver Lake and over Picture Rock Pass. After winding down the south side of the pass, watch for a sign announcing Ana Reservoir and a paved road leading east. If you reach the town of Summer Lake, you have missed the turn-off. Follow the paved road about a mile to a signed gravel road leading south a short distance to Ana Reservoir. As you reach the reservoir, stay to the right and cross over the dam. Once you cross the dam, turn left and follow the dirt/gravel road along the bluffs above the river. You can stop anywhere and hike down to the stream. To reach the lower end of the river, within Summer Lake Wildlife Management Area, follow Hwy. 31 to the north end of the little town of Summer Lake. Turn east on River Ranch Road and drive about three miles to the river.

The little Ana River offers spring-creek fishing for rainbows in a unique desert/scrubland setting near Summer Lake.

Ana Reservoir.

FRANK AMATO PHOTO

Ana Reservoir

Located just north of the town of Summer Lake, 60-acre Ana Reservoir is known primarily for its hybrid bass fishery (striped bass/white bass hybrids). Gear fishermen who have the bass figured out do most of their fishing in late winter and early spring. Ana also produces some nice rainbow trout and offers strong early season Chironomid hatches. The rainbows are planted at legal size to prevent them from being gobbled up by abundant chubs (the primary food source for the hybrid bass, which can exceed 10 pounds). Holdover rainbows, though not particularly common, reach 16 to 18 inches. Owing to its spring sources, Ana Reservoir remains ice-free during winter and is little affected by drought. See Ana River above for directions.

Chewaucan River

A good bet for wild and hatchery rainbows up to 14 inches (averaging eight to ten inches), the Chewaucan River flows south to north out of the mountains near Paisley, south of Summer Lake, in Lake County. The Chewaucan fishes best from midsummer through mid-autumn, but can rise and discolor rapidly following summer thunderstorms.

Access is best on the lower 12 miles, from Paisley up to the downstream extent of Coffeepot Flats. This entire reach is paralleled by a good road (Forest Route 33), which turns west out of Paisley. At Coffeepot Flats, the road swings up and away from the river and from here on up to the headwaters, the river flows through extensive private ranch property. A nice campground (Marster's Springs) is situated on the river about nine miles from Paisley.

Chewaucan River.

JIM SCHOLLMEYER PHOTO

Caddis and stonefly hatches predominate during summer; hoppers abound by mid-July. Most of the time, your favorite attractor dry fly will fool plenty of fish and only on occasion must you resort to matching a hatch. During spring and early summer, when flows run high, water color may dictate your choice of tactics: high, clear water begs big dry flies while high off-color water is better suited to streamers and stonefly nymphs.

Thompson Valley Reservoir

Sprawling Thompson Valley Reservoir covers more than 2,000 acres at full pool and can provide fair to excellent fishing for 12- to 22-inch rainbows. Lahontan cutthroat are stocked as well and an increasingly abundant supply of smallmouth bass are available owing to an illegal planting of these fish sometime during the early 1990s.

The reservoir occupies a timbered valley in the Fremont National Forest about 13 miles south of the town of Silver Lake, in Lake County. Forest Route 28 turns south from Silver Lake and FR27 heads south from Hwy. 31 just west of town. Both roads lead to Thompson Valley Reservoir. FR27 reaches the west side of the reservoir and FR28 leads to the east side; south of the reservoir, FR3142 connects the two primary roads. Access is good all around the lake and most anglers launch boats or float tubes at the campgrounds: Thompson Campground is located on the north arm of the reservoir and is accessed off FR27. East Bay Campground lies on the northeast corner and is reached from FR28.

Thompson Valley Reservoir is shallow throughout, reaching a maximum depth of only about 30 feet. Its fertile waters grow trout quickly. The best fishing occurs from mid-spring through early summer and from mid-September into November.

Duncan Reservoir

A small desert reservoir near the town of Silver Lake, Duncan provides fair to good fishing for fast-growing rainbows. Given a few years of good water supply, this turbid 35-odd-acre reservoir can grow trout to 20 inches. Follow Hwy. 31 east out of Silver Lake and watch for a signed turn-off to the south about five miles out of town (near the power lines). A gravel road leads about six miles up to the reservoir (after leaving the highway, drive about a mile and then be sure to turn right at the only intersection). Unimproved campsites are available around the reservoir.

Sid's Reservoir

A small, turbid reservoir capable of growing 20-inch rainbows in a hurry, Sid's or Sid Luce Reservoir, defines remote. The reservoir is situated in a shallow bowl atop a broad, low plateau about 10 air miles west of the little Warner Valley town of Plush. The route into Sid's takes you through the Fitzgerald Ranch, whose turn-off is just north of Plush. Included in the

Spaulding Reservoir is one of Southeast Oregon's most remote trout waters.

slow ride in are a half dozen gates (leave each one as you found it, either open or closed), two creekbed crossings, and lots of bone-jarring bumps. If you brave the road, you won't have time to enjoy the scenery because the white-knuckled driver will be busy dodging sharp rocks and the terrorized passenger will be too busy ricocheting off the truck's ceiling. If the road shows any sign of mud or if either of the creeks runs brown, I'd recommend abandoning the effort; never try to approach from the north, where you must cross Honey Creek, which has sucked up trucks in the past. By now it should be obvious that this is no place for your Lincoln Town Car. Once you cross the second creek (Colvin) you've got it licked. The reservoir sits off to your right, just east of the power lines.

Spaulding Reservoir

One of Oregon's most remote desert reservoirs, Spaulding is located in Sage Hen Canyon, north of Hwy. 140 and Guano Rim and south of Beatty's Butte. The little town of Adel lies some 30 air miles to the west. Like most desert reservoirs, Spaulding is often turbid and wind-lashed. Its fertile waters grow trout quickly, however, and 20-inch trout are available during years of good water supply. Access is by Beatty's Butte Road, which turns north off Hwy. 140 at the base of Guano Rim, just before the highway climbs up Doherty Slide and heads for Nevada. Follow the road north along Guano Rim until you see a weather-worn sign pointing east to Spaulding. After turning east, be careful as the first mile of the road can be very troublesome when wet.

Winter-like scene during May.

Playing a large trout.

FRANK AMATO PHOTO

FRANK AMATO PHOTO

FRANK AMATO PHOTO

Checking out Deep Creek.

Deep Creek

A desert stream that originates in the Crane Mountain area southeast of Lakeview, Deep Creek empties into the Warner Valley near Adel. One reach of the creek flows alongside Hwy. 140 west of Adel, but the better trout water is found to the southwest, where the creek flows through a more-or-less roadless canyon for several miles. Wild redband rainbows in this reach are aggressive to the dry fly when the creek runs clear (usually by midsummer and often during the winter and early spring) and they can reach 18 inches. Eight- to 14-inch redbands are more typical.

Until recently a two-fish limit was in effect on the canyon reaches of this delicate desert stream, but 1997 regulations omitted this rule and opened Deep Creek to general bag limits. Let's hope that the stream's isolation is its savior from overharvest and in the meantime, a few letters to the game commission might be in order.

Luckily, access to the canyon section is difficult and requires a rugged drive over backroads and in many reaches a fairly substantial walk. A long day walking and fishing will allow you to cover plenty of water. Before venturing off, get a copy of the BLM's South Half Lakeview Resource Area Recreation Guide (available from the BLM office in Lakeview).

Upstream of the canyon, the creek flows for almost five miles through Big Valley, and above the valley, the headwaters gather from several branches and tumble down toward Deep Creek Campground, located just off Forest Route 3915. The Big Valley section also provides good fishing most years, although it flows primarily through private property. If in doubt about land ownership, seek permission or check with the BLM in Lakeview.

Malheur Reservoir

One of the largest of the eastern Oregon trout reservoirs, Malheur Reservoir spans almost 1,400 acres but averages less than 20 feet in depth. Hatchery-born fingerling rainbows reach 10 inches by fall and 14 to 16 inches by their second spring. Fat, 20-inch rainbows are available during good years. A few native redbands wander in from the upper watershed. During years of good water supply, float-tubers will find this reservoir to be one of the top producers in eastern Oregon.

Spring and fall are best at Malheur Reservoir, which is rich in all the usual trout foods found in the desert reservoirs. Chironomids, including bloodworm midges, comprise the primary hatch activity, especially during the spring. Late spring and early summer brings lots of water beetle activity and a damsel emergence. Leeches, scuds and snails abound and are all heavily preyed upon by the trout.

This is good float-tube water, with lots of near-shore shallows where trout cruise morning and evening. Like most desert reservoirs, warm water temperatures during summer (along with the irrigation drawdown) make for poor fishing. An improved boat ramp is located near the dam, but no other amenities are available. Rough camping is available near the dam and close to the access roads. Bring your own water, shade, firewood, etc. Malheur is heavily fished during good water years, but fishing generally holds up well. During the fall, when crowds are hard to find, fly anglers will find Malheur at its best.

Malheur Reservoir is located a few miles north of Highway 26, about halfway between the communities of Brogan and Ironside. Willow Creek Road (gravel) reaches the reservoir from either town. Other routes lead in from I-84 to the north and east. Use care during wet weather and early in the spring as the roads near the reservoir can get sticky.

Thief Valley Reservoir

Located on the Powder River north of Baker City and a few miles east of I-84, sprawling Thief Valley Reservoir offers good fishing for rainbows during years of good water supply. Spring and fall provide the best

The Elkhorn Range dominates the skyline west of Thief Valley Reservoir.

opportunities for trout that commonly reach 16 inches and which can exceed 20 inches, feeding on a rich diet of scuds, water beetles, Chironomids, leeches, snails and other organisms. During high-water years, good fly angling lasts into July.

To reach Thief Valley, take Exit 285 off I-84 (the North Powder Exit). Turn east off the freeway and follow the main road through the little town of North Powder. About five miles from the freeway, turn right on Government Gulch Lane, then drive about two miles to a right turn over the railroad tracks. Cross the tracks, and continue another three miles to the top of a high summit from which the reservoir is visible. Follow the road on down to the county park on the reservoir's east bank, where you will find a good ramp, several good rough launches and ample camping space. For a slightly longer, but slightly less bumpy, route, continue past the turn-off for Governemnt Gulch Road for about two miles and turn right on Telocaset Road, which leads about two miles to the railroad crossing. Included at Thief Valley are pit toilets, fire pits and barbecue pits. Shade and protection from the wind are both at a premium.

A shallow bay reaches to the east just to the left of the access road as you approach the camping area. Early and late in the season, when the wind stays down, trout cruise in surprisingly shallow water in the bay, looking for scuds and water beetles. Also, the shallow areas just off the camping area and along the northeast shoreline offer excellent float-tube prospects. If you have a boat, the reservoir's upper end can be productive as well. Wade fishing is often possible, especially during the morning and evening along gently sloping banks.

Chironomid hatches occur during the spring and early summer, although you can't count on a good hatch every day. *Callibaetis* mayflies appear in limited numbers by late April and water beetles become increasingly active as spring progresses. Most of the time, searching patterns and leech imitations will take plenty of fish. Among the most productive springtime tactics is to use a two-fly rig with a Black Leech or Woolly Bugger as the lead fly and a size 10 Zug Bug, bead-head Zug Bug or Prince Nymph as a trailer.

Powder River

The Powder River is an expansive river system that flows in a big, exaggerated S-curve from the Blue Mountains west of Baker easterly to the Snake River at Brownlee Reservoir near Richland. Despite its 130-mile course, the Powder offers only a few sections of interest to serious fly anglers. Chief among these is the tailwater immediately below Thief Valley Reservoir Dam.

The dam is located on the south end of the reservoir (the landowner allows access). Just before you reach the camping area at Thief Valley, watch for a rough dirt road that turns left. Beware of wet conditions. Fishing picks up as soon as outflow from the reservoir clears during the spring. Rainbows up to 20 or more inches are available and the average fish runs about 14 inches. Weighted streamers, fished down-and-across

A cattle drive can slow the angler down.

will tempt these beautiful, fat rainbows, as will weighted nymphs of various kinds. Dry-fly enthusiasts can count on caddis hatches around dusk between late spring and early autumn; hopper fishing picks up by mid-summer during years of high flow.

Until recently, regulations allowed anglers to kill only one trout over 14 inches, but this rule was changed in 1997 and now the meat fishermen can keep a limit of large trout from the Powder. The effect on the fishery remains to be seen. In addition, the Powder is heavily degraded by cattle grazing and water diversion. During drought years, the fishery quite literally dries up, only to be restocked by escapement from Thief Valley Reservoir when water levels return to normal. Despite these problems, the tailwater fishery can be excellent at times, with healthy, fat rainbows the prize.

Below Thief Valley Reservoir, the Powder flows about 12 miles through a small, rather remote canyon. Here the river is designated as wild and scenic, a title which has had little impact on water/land management practices or public access problems. The upper two miles of this reach offers the best fishing. Unfortunately, access is difficult, with the ranch owner on the northeast side offering the only public easement. Below the canyon, the river enters Keating Valley where private property again limits access. Extensive water diversions and water-quality problems make this stretch of little interest.

Downstream of Keating Valley, an accessible and underappreciated section of the river flows along State Route 86 west of Richland. As you follow the river through a gentle canyon in this reach, watch for any areas of strong current and white-capped riffles. These well-oxygenated areas hold rainbows up to 16 inches or so, although the average fish spans nine to 14 inches. The pools and slow runs in this section are full of smallmouth bass and squawfish (both of which will eat dry flies).

To reach the Thief Valley tailwater section, follow the direction to the reservoir given under that listing. The downstream reaches are accessible via Hwy. 86, which turns east of I-84 at Baker City (Exit 302). At Exit 298 farther north, Hwy. 203 (Medical Springs Highway) heads northeast, crossing the river at the top of Keating Valley.

Another productive reach of the Powder flows out of Phillips Reservoir southwest of Baker. Follow Route 7 southwest from town some 15 miles up to Mason Dam. From the west, follow Hwy. 26 out of John Day and cross over Dixie Summit, turning left on Route 7 at Austin Junction. Water flows and clarity determine the quality of the fishery here. Trout average smaller than those below Thief Valley, but rainbows to 16 inches inhabit the tailwater reach. Camping is available adjacent to the dam and farther west at Union Creek.

Anthony Lakes Area

Among the most striking and beautiful landscapes in northeastern Oregon, the Anthony Lakes area lies in the heart of the Elkhorn Mountains northwest of Baker. Anthony Lake itself is heavily fished and contains brook trout and rainbows. However, some of the more out-of-the-way hike-in lakes in the area offer more solitude and good fishing. The Wallowa-Whitman National Forest Map (south half) shows these lakes. Most are ice-free by mid-July. Easiest access is from North Powder: Leave I-84 at Exit 285 and head west. Other primitive forest roads southwest of North Powder lead to access points for the hike-in lakes between Anthony Lakes area and Elkhorn Ridge to the south. Consult the national forest map.

Brownlee Reservoir

Located on the Snake River above Hells Canyon, Brownlee Dam backs the river up into a 14,000-acre pool teeming with smallmouth bass, crappie, catfish and other species. Its smallmouth can reach more than 20 inches and crappie to 12 inches or more are common.

The crappie are most available during the late-spring spawning season when they stage over shale bottoms in shallow water. The best time extends from mid-May through mid- to late June. You can drive along the access road on the Oregon side of the reservoir and take your pick of accessible shallows, although there is private land along parts of the

Largemouth bass.

shore. When the crappie spawn begins, smallmouth bass move in to feed on the fry, giving you the best of both worlds in one location. Early morning and evening are the best times to find bass in the shallows.

For the most part, the reservoir is easy to fish from shore. Still, a float tube or small boat allows you to fish along the drop-offs and anchored structure installed by ODFW. In addition, a float tube gets you into water deep enough for taking catfish on a fly and the reservoirs cats can reach more than 20 inches. In places, large rainbow trout provide a nice

Smiling angler with a nice Brownlee crappie.

surprise; largemouth bass, bluegill and yellow perch are all available as well.

Crappie and smallmouth bass, along with catfish and perch, abound between Huntington and Swede's Landing, along the Snake River Road that accesses the reservoir. The Powder River Arm, below Richland is a good place to try for catfish and big rainbows. Downstream from the Powder River Arm the reservoir's Oregon shoreline is accessible only by boat unless you want to make a near-suicidal climb into the canyon from the rims southeast from Halfway.

Otherwise, easiest access is from the town of Huntington for the south (upper) end of the reservoir, and Richland on the Powder River Arm. Highway 86 leads to Richland from Baker City and Interstate 84 leads southeast to the Huntington Exit (345). You can launch a small craft (tubes, pontoons, car-toppers) just about anywhere and launching facilities are located both at Richland and along the main reservoir north of Huntington (Spring Recreational Site and Swede's Landing).

Williamson River

The Williamson River ranks among Oregon's most renowned fly-fishing destinations. The river's large wild rainbows migrate up from Klamath Lake during the summer, giving fly anglers a shot at fish that will average at least 18 to 22 inches in length and sometimes reach more than 15 pounds. Despite the large fish, the Williamson has a major downfall where fly anglers are concerned: The vast majority of the river flows through private property where access from shore is impossible.

Nonetheless, for anglers willing to stick to the public access areas or float parts of the Williamson, the large rainbows arriving from Klamath Lake provide ample excitement assuming you are willing to spend most of your time fishing large streamers and nymphs. The Williamson hosts some impressive hatches, including its famed emergences of big *Hexagenia* and *Siphlonurus* (gray drake) mayflies along with blue-winged olives, pale morning duns and Tricos. Unfortunately, the big migratory rainbows don't always respond to the hatches.

The legendary Polly Rosborough fishing the Williamson.

The Head of the Williamson, where the river's natal springs bubble from the ground.

Instead, they often act more like steelhead and biologists suggest that these trout migrate into the river to escape warm lake temperatures and perhaps to spawn in the Williamson and its tributaries. In any case, the fish indeed act more like steelhead much of the time, more willing to chase streamers fished sub-surface than to rise steadily for often-abundant surface foods. Whatever the specific reasons for the behavior of these trout, anglers headed for the Williamson should go prepared to fish big streamers and nymphs in addition to being ready to cover rises with dry flies.

The Williamson is a lengthy river system, originating from spring sources on the eastern edge of the Winema National Forest near the Klamath/Lake County line. The Upper Williamson flows south to north through an extensive series of large meadows before entering Klamath Marsh about eight miles east of Hwy. 97, due east from Crater Lake. The river disappears into the broad expanse of the marsh, but re-emerges as a trickle almost 10 miles to the south, now flowing in a southerly direction

roughly parallel to Hwy. 97. Numerous spring flows contribute their waters to form the Lower Williamson. The highway crosses the lower river south of the little town of Chiloquin—long-time home of the Williamson's most noted angler, the late E.H. "Polly" Rosborough.

In reality, the upper and lower parts of the Williamson constitute two different rivers: The big migratory rainbows from Klamath Lake inhabit the lower river during the summer. Otherwise, this portion of the stream is rather lacking in resident adult rainbows, although some big browns live around the confluence of the Sprague River. Hence, the prime season on the Lower Williamson coincides with the run of fish from Klamath Lake:

Upper Williamson River.

Late June or early July through September. Above the marsh, the trout population is comprised of resident wild rainbows and brook trout, both of which can reach 20 inches or more, but average quite a bit smaller.

Parts of the upper river flow through national forest lands, but don't venture out without a copy of the Winema National Forest Map or you will have all kinds of trouble figuring out the patchwork pattern of private and public property. From Head of The River Campground, where the springs bubble forth, Forest Road 4648 roughly follows the river from a distance on the east—and I do mean roughly, as a drive down this road will keep your white knuckles glued to the wheel. Be sure to have your alignment checked afterward; check the alignment on your vehicle, too.

The better choices for most of the public lands are the spur roads off Forest Primary Route 49, which arrives at the river from the west and crosses it (on private property). The Winema National Forest Map shows which spur roads lead to the river's public reaches. (FR49 heads east off Silver Lake Highway, Route 676, a few miles east of Klamath Marsh.)

Except for a quarter mile of river at the springs, there is no public property (and no access except for guests of Yamsi Ranch) for the first seven or eight miles of river. Then the river begins to weave its way in and out of the national forest for eight or ten miles before again entering extensive private ranch holdings. In any event, those willing to ferret out the public lands on the upper river can find both solitude and good fishing, including some fine dry-fly action during strong mayfly hatches.

Below Klamath Marsh, the lower river flows for almost 15 miles through entirely private lands before again entering the Winema National Forest south of Kirk and north of Collier Memorial (north of Chiloquin). The road to Kirk Bridge is easy to miss, turning off Hwy. 97 about seven miles north of Collier Park. Kirk Bridge is notable only in that it demonstrates dramatically how quickly the Lower Williamson grows from virtually nothing to one of the West's largest spring creeks. You would be hard-pressed to believe that the tiny trickle flowing under Kirk Bridge (which is only one step removed from a culvert) is the same river whose wide meanders dominate the valley only a few miles downstream.

In fact, in the reaches below Kirk Bridge, the Williamson begins to gather the flows from many spring-fed tributaries. Several of these contribute their waters in the canyon below Kirk Bridge and by the time the stream reaches Williamson River Campground a few miles below, it has become a modest river. Then, at Collier Park, the cold rush of Spring Creek joins the Williamson and a major river is born.

About three river miles below Williamson River Campground, the river again flows through private property all the way to Klamath Lake. Bank access in this long reach is limited to just a few places, among them the popular public access near the Blue Hole below the Chiloquin Airport (airstrip would be more accurate). A three-mile float takes you down to Rapids Cafe or Water Wheel RV Park just above the Hwy. 97 Bridge (these are both private fee ramps). Williamson River Resort (at the Modoc

Point Highway bridge) offers access to the slough-like waters of the Williamson just above its confluence with Klamath Lake. Boaters looking for a longer float, can launch at points upstream and take-out here, but you will need a motor for the lower end of the trip.

The other popular all-day float is from Collier Park down to the county park. Collier is located along Hwy. 97 north of Chiloquin and is hard to miss. To find the county park, follow Hwy. 97 to the South Chiloquin Exit, turn east and watch for the county park sign on your left.

The Williamson offers several hatches of note: Giant yellow mayflies (*Hexagenia limbata*) and gray drakes (*Siphlonurus*) begin hatching mid- to late June. The "Hex hatch," when it is on, is a sight to behold. Around dusk, the huge mayflies—some two inches long including the tails—begin hatching and on some evenings, the trout respond en masse to an abundance of these bugs.

The gray drakes, sometimes called "black drakes," are nearly as large but offer a different scenario. The hatch peaks during July, but the emergence itself is of little consequence to the angler because the nymphs migrate to shore and crawl out in the relative safety of the shore-line margins. The spinner fall, on the other hand, is a significant event. On sunny days, the spinners appear around dusk; cloudy, cool weather brings them out earlier. On some nights they get so heavy that fishing is virtually a waste of time.

Other common mayflies include *Baetis* (blue-winged olives), which can hatch just about any time, pale morning duns (June-July), Tricos (July-September), green drakes (June) and speckled-wing duns (*Callibaetis*) (June-August). Myriad caddis are present as well, with the best hatches usually occurring in the riffle sections. The October caddis (*Dicosmoecus*) is an orange-bodied giant that appears during fall. Early in the season, stoneflies hatch in and near the riffles and rapids. Finally, terrestrial insects, including ants, beetles and hoppers, abound all along the river.

Despite the great hatches, the migratory trout in the lower river are renowned for ignoring the surface. Instead, nymphs and streamers provide much of the action on the Lower Williamson. Effective streamer patterns are diverse and numerous, but you can't go wrong with flies such as the Bunny Leech, Woolly Bugger, Marabou Muddler, Zonker and Matuka, all in various colors, including black, brown, olive, claret and purple. The other choice is to scale down with smaller nymphs (size 8-14) and tiny streamers (size 8-10), fishing either on a sinking or sink-tip line and working the fly very slowly by casting up and across, allowing the fly to sink and then twitching it back.

If you don't own a drift boat, you might consider hiring one of the many guides who work the Williamson. Check with Williamson River Anglers, owned by Steve and Judy Caruthers, located on the river at the Hwy. 97 bridge south of Chiloquin. They can also put you in touch with Yamsi Ranch, a popular private ranch that caters to fly anglers on the Upper Williamson River.

A Sampling of Polly Rosborough's Williamson River Patterns

Big Yellow May Nymph

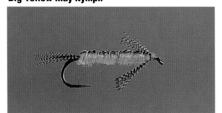

Hook:	3XL nymph/streamer, size 6-8
Thread:	Yellow
Tail:	Lemon wood duck fibers
Rib:	Large yellow thread
Shellback:	Lemon wood duck fibers
Body:	Yellow wool
Legs:	Lemon wood duck fibers
Wingcase:	Lemon wood duck fibers

Dark Caddis

Hook:	Dry fly, size 6-8
Body:	Burnt orange dubbing
Rib:	Dark brown hackle, palmered through body
Wing:	Dark natural deer hair
Hackle:	Dark brown

Little Yellow Stone

Hook:	2XL dry fly, size 10-12
Tail:	Crimson hackle, clipped short for egg sack then pale yellow grizzly hackle fibers
Rear Hackle:	Pale yellow grizzly hackle
Body:	Chartreuse rabbit dubbing
Rib:	Yellow thread
Front Hackle:	Pale yellow grizzly hackle

Golden Stone Wet

Hook: 2XL or 3XL nymph/streamer hook
Tail: Mallard flank, dyed gold
Body: Antique-gold wool
Rib: Antique-gold thread
Hackle: Antique-gold dyed hen hackle then gold-dyed mallard flank
Wing: Gold-dyed bucktail

Dark Stone Wet

Hook: 2XL or 3XL nymph/streamer hook
Tail: Brown turkey fibers from body feather
Body: Tangerine wool
Rib: Gray thread
Hackle: Dark furnace hen hackle, undersized
Wing: Dark brown bucktail
Head: Band of hot orange floss at base of wing

Golden Stone Nymph

Hook: 3XL streamer, size 4-6
Tail: Teal flank
Rib: Large golden-yellow thread
Body: Antique-gold yarn
Shellback: Teal flank fibers
Legs: Teal flank fibers
Wingcase: Teal flank

Casual Dress

Hook: 2XL or 3XL streamer hook, size 4-10
Tail: Muskrat fur, with guard hairs, tied short
Body: Muskrat fur, loop-dubbed
Thorax: Muskrat fur with guard hairs
Head: Black ostrich herl

Black Drake Nymph

Hook: Nymph hook, size 8-10
Tail: Guinea fibers
Body: Beaver fur dubbing with guard hairs, loop-dubbed
Wingcase: Black ostrich herl
Legs: Guinea fibers

Muskrat

Hook: 2XL nymph/streamer, size 6-16
Body: Muskrat fur, loop-dubbed
Throat: Guinea fibers
Head: Black ostrich herl

Sprague River

A 100-mile-long tributary of the Williamson, the Sprague River offers good fishing in its own right. Its lower few miles hold some large, migratory rainbows and a few browns, with the short reach between Chiloquin Dam and the Williamson River closed to bait-fishing. Best access to the mouth of the Sprague is by boat from the Williamson, but walk-in anglers can gain access in the town of Chiloquin: Take either exit (north or south) off Hwy. 97 and head into Chiloquin. You will cross the Williamson River and then come to an intersection in downtown Chiloquin. Turn right and head straight through town and into a residential district (2nd Avenue). Continue back to the high school and follow a gravel road leading toward the old mill, behind the school's football and baseball fields.

Above the dam and up to Braymill, a few miles east of Chiloquin, much of the river flows through National Forest property. Above its mouth, the river's course follows a five-mile-long horseshoe bend around Chiloquin Ridge, eventually picking up Sprague River Highway east of town. Much of the river within this five miles flows through Winema National Forest lands and is accessible to walk-in anglers. The best access is from Chiloquin Ridge Road about a mile east of town on the highway (the turn-off is at the Pacific Power sub-station). Turn right off the highway, cross the bridge and drive until you reach the last house on the river. The road will swing away from the river, but you can park and walk in.

During summer, you will find lots of shallow, warm, weedy flats. The trout congregate in the deeper sections: A few pools and deep runs and below riffles. Hopper season can offer some good dry-fly action. Evening caddis hatches occur with regularity as well.

Above Braymill and then all the way to Beatty far to the east, the Sprague is largely surrounded by private ranch lands with little or no bank access. Some three miles of river west of Lone Pine (seven miles east of Braymill) are accessible, mostly along the highway. Largemouth bass inhabit the slow, meandering, middle reaches of the Sprague in Sprague River Valley, from Lone Pine up to Beatty.

The headwater tributaries of the Sprague (the North Fork and South Fork) offer good fishing for small trout. The South Fork features brown trout, brook trout and some rainbows, all wild. The latter predominate in the North Fork, with some browns in the lower reaches. While the fish average on the small side, an occasional brown in the South Fork might reach 20 inches. Both forks harbor native bull trout in limited numbers and these are fully protected and must be released unharmed.

Both forks run through public and private property, so peruse a copy of the Fremont National Forest Map and knock on a door if you're not sure about access. Once you get to the upper stretches of both streams, public lands predominate.

Hwy. 140 follows the South Fork through Bly on the way up to Quartz Mountain Pass. The best reaches require a fair hike. The North Fork is more accessible in its upper reaches, being paralleled by FR3372 along the eastern edge of the Gearhart Mountain Wilderness. Be sure to consult the National Forest map. Two nice campgrounds are located on the North Fork (Sandhill Crossing and Lee Thomas). Best fishing for wild redbands is above Sandhill Crossing. If you're spending any time in the area, be sure to explore some of the other small streams, especially those that require a short hike.

Sycan River

A beautiful mountain stream in its upper reaches (above the ZX Ranch), the Sycan offers good fishing for small rainbow trout and brook trout. Most fish span six to 10 inches, but a few 14- to 20-inch trout, always found in the deeper pools and runs, can make things interesting. Most reaches of the river are lightly fished for several reasons: First, the Sycan competes for attention with much more prominent area waters like the Williamson, Sprague and Klamath rivers and Klamath Lake. Second, access to much of the Sycan is by way of lengthy and often rough backroads in the Fremont and Winema national forests.

The Sycan's headwaters gather from the timbered hills on the west side of Winter Ridge about 10 miles west (as the crow flies) of Paisley. Immediately to the south is the extensive Chewaucan River drainage. The upper Sycan winds a northwesterly course through the Fremont

National Forest and is accessed primarily by spur roads leading off Forest Primary Route 28, Forest Primary Route 30 and Forest Road 3239. All told the upper river offers almost 25 miles of tumbling pocket-water, gliding runs, undercut banks and plunge-pools.

At the bottom of this upper reach, the river flows under FR3239 and into the expansive Sycan Marsh, virtually all of which is owned by several large ranches, including the ZX. Below the marsh, the Sycan again enters public property and forms the border of the Fremont and Winema national forests. At this point, brown trout enter the picture as the river's gradient lessens. The lower river flows southwesterly and then due south through forested bottoms and meadows. The lower 10 miles of the river again flow through private property and the Sycan empties into the Sprague River near the little town of Beatty, located on Hwy. 140 about 40 miles northeast of Klamath Falls.

From the marsh downstream, access to the Sycan is more difficult than in the upper river. Nowhere is the river followed for any length by good roads. Several National Forest Primary Routes will get you to the area and a series of secondary and primitive roads approach the river throughout its length in the national forest. Floaters can put-in at the river crossing below the marsh on FR27 and make the 12-mile drift down to Teddy Powers Meadows, which is accessed by turning north on County Rd. 1193 at Beatty and driving north to a left turn onto FR347 (which crosses the river). Before venturing out, obtain a copy of the Fremont National Forest Map from the Forest Service or from a local map dealer.

The lower Sycan, from Sycan Marsh downstream, offers highly secluded fishing for those willing to make the effort to first get to the river and then to walk for a while. The trout average quite a bit larger than those in the upper river, with browns and rainbows of 14 to 20 inches available. However, due to an extensive history of heavy water use for agriculture, the lower river doesn't offer a particularly dense population of trout. Nonetheless, the chance for big trout and ample solitude make for an attractive package.

On the lower river, best fishing occurs during late spring and early summer unless high snowpack results in heavy run-off. During the summer, fishing slows as water levels plunge and water temperatures rise, but autumn brings renewed action. The upper river fishes best from midsummer through mid-fall. A selection of basic dry flies, including ant and hopper patterns, will do the trick and on the lower river, large streamer patterns can draw big browns out of their hiding places, especially early and late in the day.

Klamath River

Southern Oregon's Klamath River derives its nutrient base from the fertile waters of Upper Klamath Lake and its downstream reservoirs. The Klamath—its 38 miles in Oregon at least—is really three different rivers, each with a unique character. Together the three sections offer quality year-round trout fishing.

The productive water begins below Keno Dam, near the town of Keno on Route 66 west of Klamath Falls. The six-mile reach from Keno Dam down to Boyle Reservoir, best in its upper three to four miles, offers wild rainbows that average around 14 inches and frequently go 16 to 20 inches with a few larger still.

The Keno Dam stretch is amazingly fertile water, with dense populations of stoneflies, caddis and baitfish. Yet the trout rarely rise for dry flies despite voluminous hatches that envelope the river at times. Instead these fish gorge beneath the surface in the heavy, boulder-strewn waters. Large, weighted nymphs and big streamer patterns are the most successful flies. Dedicated Keno-reach anglers will happen upon the occasional large trout feeding on adult stoneflies or caddisflies, but don't count on it.

A summer closure (June 15 through October 1) restricts fishing to the fall through spring months and offers fish safe haven during the stressful high water-temperature period during summer. Discharges from Keno Dam restrict the fishing even further, requiring that traveling anglers call ahead to check water levels (Pacific Power, 1-800-547-1501). Flows below 1,000 cfs are optimal, but not necessarily the rule.

A rugged part of the Klamath River.

This section of river is best accessed from the Pacific Power Recreation Site immediately west of Keno on Hwy. 66. The recreational site includes a fee campground along with easy access to the river below Keno Dam. Several pullouts along Hwy. 66 west of the PPL site lead to precipitous trails that plunge into the deep canyon. If you access the river from these steep bushwhacker's trails, make sure your affairs are in order ahead of time.

For the first four miles below Boyle Dam, the Klamath offers similar water but with small trout. However, because of their willingness to clobber dry flies and because of the lack of pressure on the four-mile stretch below Boyle Dam, this area has become my favorite. The trout rarely exceed a foot in length, but they are scrappy devils whose appetite for dry flies will endear them to most anglers.

Early morning and evening fishing is most productive during the summer catch-and-release season, which runs from June 15 to September 30. June offers good stonefly hatches. Salmonflies and golden stoneflies both make an appearance and the rainbows are quick to take notice. By early July, caddis dominate the hatches, with good evening rises the rule. Hoppers can be nothing short of abundant by August and trout will rise eagerly for imitations, especially during early evening just as the sun leaves the water.

Nearly as abundant during the summer are rattlesnakes and stinging nettle. Watch your step and be careful which plants you barge through to get at the water.

To access the river below Boyle Dam, follow Hwy. 66 west out of Keno approximately six miles to Boyle Reservoir. Follow the highway across a narrow reach of the reservoir and drive another 1.7 miles until you see a gravel road on the left. Typically the road is marked by a sign announcing Boyle Dam, but last time I checked the sign was missing. Turn left off Hwy. 66 and proceed about 1/2 mile to the third left turn off the main road. You will wind down a short incline where a big flume and a bridge crosses the narrow river. Instead of crossing the bridge, turn right on the road that runs along the cement flume above the river. From there you have almost two miles of water, several pullouts and numerous steep, semi-treacherous climbs down to the river. This access road meets up with the main gravel road at the lower spill-way and from here you have another two miles of good (albeit steep) access to the river until you reach Boyle Substation.

Fishing a beautiful section of the Klamath River.

The third distinct reach of the Klamath begins at the substation where the river doubles or triples in size with the additional waters from the huge flumes being routed back into the stream channel. From here to the California border, the Klamath is a big, rowdy river with a good population of nice rainbows, many of which span 12 to 16 inches. Unlike the four-mile reach between the dam and the substation, this lower part of the river is truly wild water where wading anglers will want to take extreme care. A rough gravel road provides good access to the river all the way to the state line.

Anglers in search of remote waters will enjoy the Klamath below Boyle Substation, where about eight miles of tumultuous river flows through a massive canyon cloaked in firs, oaks and mountain mahogany. Stoneflies hatch in impressive numbers during early summer and caddis hatches can be nothing short of awesome. As with any section of the Klamath, expect some daily fluctuations in water levels due to power generation schedules.

As a package, the three reaches of Oregon's Klamath River offer year-round opportunities for wild rainbows. You can choose what you like: Autumn and spring fishing for big trout below Keno Dam, great dry-fly action for small rainbows in the pocket water between Boyle Dam and the substation or remote and untamed action on the furious waters towards the California border.

Upper Klamath Lake

Covering more than 60,000 surface acres, Upper Klamath Lake is the largest lake in Oregon. Despite its intimidating size, however, this shallow, fertile lake supports a thriving population of fast-growing rainbow trout that commonly exceed 20 inches in length. Six-pound fish are barely noteworthy in Klamath Lake and rainbows to 10 or 12 pounds are available in fair numbers. All are wild trout.

The lake is located just northwest of the town of Klamath Falls in south-central Oregon. Its largest tributary, the Williamson River and its outlet, the Klamath River, rank among the state's top fly waters.

Upper Klamath Lake, typically referred to simply as Klamath Lake, is replete with all the typical still-water trout foods, such as scuds, damsels, leeches and snails, but it also contains a tremendous population of chub minnows and other baitfish. These comprise a major element in the diet of the trout and in part explains why a three-year-old Klamath Lake rainbow will span about 20 inches. No surprise that streamer patterns consistently produce large fish.

Good choices for streamers include Zonkers in brown/gold, black/pearl, white/pearl, olive/gold and tan/gold; other effective streamers include the Mickey Finn, Polar Chub, Olive Matuka and Marabou Muddler. Leech patterns are always a good bet. Popular patterns include Rabbit Strip Leeches, Woolly Buggers and numerous other dressings. The Nevada Leech, listed in the fly pattern section of this book, has been a consistent producer. Good colors for leech patterns include black, olive, olive-brown, maroon and combinations thereof.

Best fishing on the lake occurs during spring and fall; summer brings high water temperatures that slow the action and force the trout to seek cool-water holes, springs and inlet areas. April, May and June are prime months during the spring. Fly anglers tend to concentrate in the northern part of the lake, including Pelican Bay, a narrow arm that extends about two miles up from the northwest corner of Klamath Lake. The narrows between Klamath and Agency lakes is another popular area, as is the Shoalwater Bay/Eagle Point area. Modoc Point, located on the east shoreline where Hwy. 97 first reaches the lake from the north, offers good fishing at times and is easily accessible, but lacks a boat ramp. Also on the east side, Hagelstein Park provides access to Ouxy Springs and Sucker Springs, both of which attract trout as water temperatures rise. The springs are located along the shoreline north of the park.

These same areas are productive in the fall as well, with fishing picking up as temperatures cool from mid- to late September through at least early November. Spring or fall, the lake is fishable by boat or float tube. A boat allows for more mobility and float-tube anglers often use a boat to transport themselves to productive areas that would otherwise call for too long a trek by tube alone. A word of caution: Serious waves can kick up in a hurry on this expansive lake, even on relatively calm days, so always keep an eye on the weather.

Fishing the Klamath below Boyle Dam.

Upper Klamath Lake is easily accessed by a network of good roads. Hwy. 97 arrives from the north and from the south and parallels the eastern shoreline for about 10 miles north of Klamath Falls. Hwy. 140 heads northwest out of Klamath Falls and follows the shoreline of Howard Bay for a couple miles and also provides access to most of the northwest end of the lake. To reach Shoalwater Bay and Eagle Point, turn northeast off the highway onto Eagle Ridge Road about 15 miles northwest of Klamath Falls. Four miles further northwest on Hwy. 140, a short spur road leads down to Odessa Creek and Odessa Campground. A few miles further up the highway, Westside Road takes off to the north, providing access to Pelican Bay and to Rocky Point Resort, where guides and rental boats are available. Public launches on the west side of Klamath Lake are located at Howard Bay (10 miles northwest of Klamath Falls), Eagle Ridge (Shoalwater Bay), Odessa Creek, Rocky Point Landing and Rocky Point Resort. An additional fee ramp is located at Harriman Lodge two miles north of Hwy. 140 off Westside Road.

Agency Lake

Like Upper Klamath Lake, Agency Lake offers big rainbows, with 18- and 20-inch fish the average. Brown trout are present as well and these too reach impressive sizes. Agency is connected to Klamath Lake to the south by a narrow channel, while the north end of the lake is fed by Wood River.

As with Upper Klamath Lake, Agency fishes best during spring, from April through early June, and during mid- to late fall. Two county parks provide good boat ramps and most of the fishing occurs in the vicinity of the parks. Both the mouth of the Wood River arm and the adjacent shoreline to the west are consistently productive and are accessed from the launch at Petric Park. On the south end of the lake, try the narrows separating Agency from Klamath Lake. A four-mile boat ride from Henzel Park on the east shore or from Pelican Bay on Klamath Lake will get you there.

Primary access to Agency Lake is from Hwy. 97 north of Klamath Falls. From the south, follow Hwy. 97 along the east shore of Klamath Lake and then turn west at Modoc Point (Modoc Point Road). The road is poorly marked, but just watch for the first road leading west as the highway leaves the shoreline of Klamath Lake. From the north, turn west at

KEN MORRISH PHOTO

Wood River.

Chiloquin onto the Chiloquin Highway (South Chiloquin Road, which is the southernmost of the two Chiloquin exits) and cross Hwy. 62 to reach Modoc Point Road. After crossing Hwy. 62, South Chiloquin Road winds its way over to Modoc Point Road near Henzel Park.

From Hwy. 97 on the south, follow Modoc Point Road six miles to Williamson River Resort and continue northwest, crossing the Williamson River. Henzel Park is on the left a short distance past the river. Modoc Point Road continues north along the east shoreline of Agency Lake, but fishing access is virtually impossible due to extensive private property.

To reach the mouth of the Wood River and Petric Park, continue north on Modoc Point Road another four miles. Arriving from the south, you will see a wide gravel road that leads to a parking area for the Wood River Wetlands Area. A half mile further north on the highway, watch for the turn-off to Petric Park, also on the left. A gravel road leads a few hundred yards down to the ramp and parking area, which are located at the end of a narrow channel. To reach the main lake, you must boat south and then west in the channel. A good gravel road leads out to the Wetlands Area, but motorized vehicles are prohibited. Float-tubers can walk or bike in.

Wood River

Locally renowned for its big browns and rainbows that hide under extensively under-cut banks, pretty little Wood River meanders through broad meadows on its north to south journey from spring sources north of Fort Klamath to Agency Lake. Now the bad news: Virtually the entire river flows through private land, so you must either knock on doors until you get permission or boat the river, which is the decidedly better choice, even though boat access is nearly as troublesome as foot access.

The Forest Service maintains a picnic area just north of the little town of Fort Klamath and boaters can put-in here and float down to Loosely Road or Weed Road, both of which offer narrow highway easements where small boats can be launched or taken out. Bear in mind, however, that a drift boat is essentially out of the question unless you have access to private property because the highway easements at Loosely and Weed roads are nothing more than eight or 10 feet of space

between the bridge guardrails and the fence lines. A small car-topper, canoe or pontoon boat can be carried in or out of the river adjacent to the bridges. Another launch point is well upstream at Kimball Park, but here too you must carry the boat to the water. From Kimball, you can float down to the Forest Service access. Weed Road, incidentally, is the last bridge access above Agency Lake, so unless you plan on motoring down the mouth of the river and up to Petric Park, you should exit at Weed Road.

Petric Park offers an opportunity to fish both Wood and Agency lake in the same outing. Just put-in at the park and motor down the canal until you reach the lake proper and the mouth of the Wood. Fish the lake during the early morning hours and then run upstream to check on the mid-morning PMD hatch.

The Wood River meanders gracefully through its wide valley, offering countless winding S-curves with deep corners and undercut banks. Other than poor access, its only downfall is the predominance of cattle grazing right down to the banks. Good hatches of pale morning duns occur during the summer; blue-winged olives emerge throughout most of the season, with the strongest hatches between May and early June and again in the fall. Look for the best hatches on cloudy days. Early morning spinner falls are common, though localized like the hatches themselves.

Perhaps the best fishing of the season on the Wood happens when the grasshoppers appear from midsummer through early fall. An abundance of hoppers and a windy day can spell great dry-fly action for big trout. When the hatches of hoppers don't occur or when the trout ignore them, try streamers. The big browns and rainbows, the latter being migrants from Agency Lake, often hide under the cut banks waiting for an opportunity to ambush some hapless minnow or sculpin.

The Wood River is managed to preserve wild, native rainbows and wild brown trout. Fishing is catch-and-release only with artificial flies or lures. The season typically runs from the end of April through the end of October. Owing to the special regulations and to the preponderance of private land, the Wood River remains one of Oregon's most unheralded trout streams and while trout densities are not particularly high, the average fish runs large. Trout of four to six pounds are average and with rainbows migrating up from super-fertile Agency Lake, trophies of 10 pounds or better are always possible.

To reach the Wood River, follow Highway 97 south from Bend or north from Klamath Falls. From the south turn west (left) at the Hwy. 62 junction just north of the Williamson River Bridge south of Chiloquin. From the north, exit Hwy. 97 at the North Chiloquin Exit, which points the way to Fort Klamath and follow this road over to Hwy. 62. Take 62 north into the Wood River Valley, which lies just a few miles northwest of Chiloquin.

The access points are found as follows: To reach Kimball Park, continue north on Hwy. 62 until you see the Fort Klamath Military Park and Museum on your left. Just past the park, the highway swings to the left and a well-signed turn-off to the right heads north three miles to Kimball Park, which offers a few nice camping spots among the conifers. The Forest Service access is located just north of Fort Klamath: Instead of turning right to reach Kimball Park, follow the highway into town, then watch for the signs as you leave the north end of this small community. Loosely Road and Weed Road both turn left off Hwy. 62. Loosely Road is two miles south of the Kimball Park turn-off and Weed Road (un-signed last time I was there) is two miles south from there (just north of the turn-off to the state fish hatchery on Crooked Creek).

Although all of the float segments of the river are quite short as the crow flies (e.g. Kimball to Fort Klamath, Fort Klamath to Loosely, Fort Klamath or Loosely to Weed Rd., Weed Rd. to Petric Park), they will consume a day when fishing is good because the river meanders constantly. At the Loosely and Weed Road bridges, parking is limited to non-existent. There is just enough room against the guardrails for one car per side. In such situations, I've always considered it good policy to check in with the nearest farmer and ask if he minds that I park at the bridge. He may not own the property, but he may have to move equipment or cattle; besides, striking up the conversation might gain you a better parking spot or perhaps even some foot access to the river.

Sevenmile Creek, Crooked Creek, Fort Creek

Fort Creek is a tributary to the Wood River, while Crooked Creek and Sevenmile Creek flow into Agency Lake. All three streams are restricted to catch-and-release, artificials-only-fishing for trout and all three can produce good-sized rainbows and browns. The entire Wood River Valley is comprised largely of private property, so anglers must seek permission to fish most of these waters. Only the diminutive upper reaches of these streams flow through National Forest land.

Fort Creek's headwater reaches are followed by a road leading north and east off Hwy. 62 just north of Klamath Junction. Brook trout and rainbows predominate and most are small. The lower reaches of Fort Creek, home to some large rainbows and browns, are inaccessible due to private resort holdings.

Nearby Crooked Creek, which more-or-less runs along Hwy. 62 south of Klamath Junction, offers fair fishing for browns, rainbows and brook trout. A nice mile-long reach of Crooked Creek flows through public property at the state fish hatchery. Watch for the hatchery signs along the highway south of Weed Road. The road leading up to the hatchery offers several pull-outs where anglers can park and walk down to the creek. Downstream from Highway 62, Crooked Creek flows through private land that has typically been accessible with permission of the nearby landowner.

The best bet is Sevenmile Creek, which originates inside the Winema National Forest west of Fort Klamath. The upper creek, within the national forest, offers fair to good fishing for brook trout and rainbows, along with a few brown trout. Once the creek flows out of the National Forest and turns southeasterly, it meanders through several miles of private property below Nicholson Road. The few miles of creek here can be good for rainbows and browns, including some large ones, if you are willing to seek permission. The last six miles of the creek are channelized into "Sevenmile Canal." Easiest access to the creek is to turn west at Fort Klamath onto Nicholson Road, which reaches the creek near Sevenmile Guard Station a few miles from town. To reach the upper stretches, cross the creek at Nicholson Road

and swing to the right on FR3334. A campground with minimal facilities is located near the headwaters at Sevenmile Marsh.

Miller Lake

Somewhat overlooked in the shadow of so many great trout lakes in Central Oregon, Miller Lake offers fair fishing for brown trout from 12 to 20-plus inches along with rainbows from eight to 16 inches, sometimes larger. All trout are stocked and natural reproduction has never been documented. The lake is not particularly rich, but the trout still manage to gain three to five inches per year.

Miller Lake's largest brown trout feed on kokanee so a large streamer pattern trolled on a sinking line might produce a fish up to six or eight pounds. Fish along the shoreline margins early and late in the day. Because brown trout are fall spawners, many fly anglers fish Miller during October, even November, when the fish cruise the near-shore shallows and attack the flies with a vengeance.

Miller Lake covers about 600 acres and is located on the east slope of the Cascades in the northwest corner of the Winema National Forest (Klamath County), about 10 air miles northeast of Diamond Lake. Sitting at an elevation of 5,630 feet, Miller Lake is usually snow-bound until June. To reach Miller Lake, take Hwy. 97 to Chemult, then turn west on Forest Road 9772 (about a mile north of town; a highway sign announces Miller Lake). The drive covers about 12 miles of gravel and leads to a Digit Point Campground on the lake's south shore.

Holbrook Reservoir

Thanks to a long-standing agreement with the property owner, 40-acre Holbrook Reservoir and its fat rainbows are available to anglers. The clear-water reservoir sits almost entirely on private land south of Hwy. 140 some 30 miles west of Lakeview in the southwestern corner of Lake County. Although no special regulations apply to Holbrook, the reservoir is isolated enough that fishing holds up despite moderate pressure from bait anglers. Rainbows reach 20 inches; 12- to 14-inch fish are common.

Holbrook offers a good boat ramp, but float-tubers can find easy bank access in many places around the lake. Chironomids and *Callibaetis* mayflies provide most of the surface action while standard attractor-type wet flies always prove effective. Good patterns include the Zug Bug, Woolly Bugger, Prince Nymph, Marabou Searcher and many others. Holbrook hosts a good population of damsels, water beetles, water boatmen, back-swimmers, leeches and scuds, so like imitations of these organisms will catch fish. Watch for water beetle activity in the shallows during spring and early summer, especially during the evening.

To reach Holbrook, follow Hwy. 140 east from Klamath Falls or west from Lakeview. The turn-off is at the top of Quartz Mountain Pass, some 12 miles east of the little community of Bly. At Quartz Mountain Pass, turn south on Forest Road 3715 and drive about five miles to a right-hand turn on FR3817, which leads a mile down to Holbrook Reservoir. Nearest camping is at Lofton Reservoir: Follow FR3715 about 1.5 miles past the turn-off to Holbrook Reservoir (FR3817) and turn left on FR013. Signs will keep you headed in the right direction. Lofton has problems with chub populations from time to time, but is still a fair producer of 10- to 14-inch rainbows.

Cottonwood Meadows Lake

This scenic 40-acre lake provides fair to good fishing for 10- to 16-inch rainbows and brook trout, especially during late spring and mid-autumn. An easy drive from Lakeview, the lake gets lots of angling pressure, but heavy stocking of fingerlings assures a constant supply of trout. Follow Hwy. 140 about 20 miles west from Lakeview and turn north at a signed turn-off on FR3870. A campground is located at the lake. The Cottonwood Creek drainage downstream from the lake, including 200-acre Cottonwood Reservoir, is closed to trout fishing to protect native redband trout whose numbers were severely reduced when Goose Lake went dry during the drought of the early 1990s.

The rugged Wallowa Mountains in Oregon's northeast corner are among the state's most impressive and picturesque ranges. Their magnitude can only be fully appreciated by an up-close view, especially from within the confines of the 294,000-acre Eagle Cap Wilderness, where ruggedly steep, timbered, granite-capped ridges hide numerous small alpine lakes teeming with trout.

Southwest and west from the Wallowas, across the valley from the Grande Ronde and Powder rivers, the Blue Mountains form eastern Oregon's most extensive range. Their centerpiece are the Elkhorn Mountains, whose sheer enormity and rugged beauty rival that of the Wallowas.

Naturally, the extensive mountains that define northeastern Oregon form the headwater drainages of many important and beautiful rivers. From the Wallowas flow the Minam, Imnaha, Lostine and Wallowa rivers. The Blue Mountains deliver the Grande Ronde, Umatilla, John Day and Malheur. All of these streams, and several others to boot, offer fisheries of significance to the fly angler, whether it be the exceptional trout fishing on the Minam, the popular steelheading available on the Grande Ronde or the renowned smallmouth bass action on the John Day.

The northeast corner of Oregon is replete with stillwater fishing as well. Several reservoirs offer fast-growing rainbow trout in waters quite similar to the desert reservoirs of the Southeast Zone and countless high lakes combine good brook trout angling with exceptional solitude and picturesque surroundings. Even warm-water opportunities abound in this region: Brownlee Reservoir on the Snake River, though administered by ODFW's Southeast Zone, is within easy reach of anglers from La Grande or Baker; it features the state's best combination smallmouth bass/crappie fishery. Both species abound in this long, fertile reservoir and both afford great sport on a fly rod.

In addition to Brownlee, warm-water enthusiasts can fish the Columbia River itself along with its many back-waters and sloughs, many of which are approachable along Interstate 84, the main artery through the region. Smallmouth bass are abundant and a variety of other warm-water species thrive in these waters.

The region's history includes the stories of Oregon's earliest peoples, who lived along the Columbia and its tributaries thousands of years ago. More recently, northeastern Oregon became Nez Perce Country and the land of famed Chief Joseph. Early white settlers included some of the first missionaries to arrive in the Northwest and not long after came the miners seeking gold in the Wallowas.

A little further to the west, the John Day River country offers a rich geological and archaeological history of its own, as demonstrated by the tremendous fossil deposits in the area and by the pictographs and other remnants of a once-thriving Native American culture. A visit to the John Day Fossil Beds is well worth the time and for those willing to look for them, the pictographs in Picture Gorge are a wonderment in themselves. Sad testimony to our times is the fact that by policy the staff who man the Fossil Beds Visitor's Center north of Picture Gorge cannot tell you where to find the beautiful pictographs, which are drawn in red ink on sheer basalt walls: In recent years, vandals have both chipped away some of the rock and sprayed graffiti over the elegant Indian designs.

Summer steelhead with lamprey scar.   FRANK AMATO PHOTO

Grand Ronde River

The most popular fly-rod steelhead stream in northeastern Oregon, and one of the most popular east of the Cascades, the Grand Ronde flows more-or-less northeasterly for more than 200 miles from its source in the Blue Mountains, through the Grand Ronde Valley, into its canyon at Elgin and Troy and then into Washington before it joins the Snake River downstream from Hells Canyon, seven miles north of the Oregon state line.

Steelhead anglers converge on the river in October and the fishing continues through December. In fact, although these are summer-run steelhead, fishing often continues right through the winter, at least when water conditions allow. Cold water between December and March forces fly anglers to fish tactics suited to typical winter steelhead angling, but the fishing can be productive. Still, the October-November season is best for those who prefer floating lines and mild weather.

The fishery extends up to the legal deadline at Meadow Creek, about half way between La Grande and Ukiah, but the river above Elgin is not particularly of interest to most of the river's serious steelhead anglers.

Meanwhile, hatchery steelhead make up a majority of the catch, with four- to eight-pound fish being typical. Much of the fly-angling pressure is concentrated around Troy, where the river is easily accessible by road. Grand Ronde Road follows the river's north bank for some 14 miles downstream from Troy and for several miles upstream as well (to the Mud Creek and Wildcat Creek boat accesses). On the south bank opposite Troy, a county road leads about a mile along the river to the ODFW ramp. The road-accessible portion of the Grand Ronde is ideal for those willing to first buy both an Oregon and Washington license and steelhead tag and second scramble up and down the banks.

Below Troy, on the Washington side, the river road eventually departs the canyon, leaving to boaters the lower 20-plus miles. The put-

Al Buhr on the Grand Ronde River.

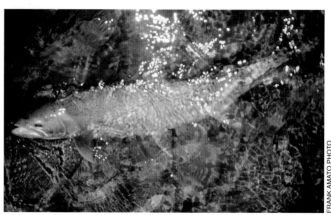

Summer-run steelhead.

in for this reach is at the Hwy. 129 bridge (or you can launch upriver at Troy) and the take-out is at the mouth, which is accessible via Snake River Road, which leads south from Clarkston, Washington. To allow adequate time for fishing, you should plan several days for this trip.

You can drift the upper water, from Wildcat Creek or from the put-in at Troy, but if you do so, make a close study of boating etiquette because in the small confines of the Grand Ronde, you will risk floating right over the water being covered by wading anglers.

Imnaha River

Among the most scenic rivers in eastern Oregon, the Imnaha originates high in the Wallowa Mountains, within the Eagle Cap Wilderness, eventually swinging to a northerly course on its long, tumultuous journey to the Snake River near Hells Canyon. The Imnaha joins the Snake just a few miles above the confluence of Idaho's mighty Salmon River. All told, the Imnaha flows some 80 miles from source to mouth.

The Imnaha offers good fishing for wild trout in most reaches and is a good choice for anglers looking for a hike-in fly-fishing experience as its upper end flows entirely through designated wilderness. The lower river even offers good fishing for smallmouth bass that have inhabited the lower reaches of most Snake River tributaries. Summer steelhead provide an additional fishery, with best prospects from October through November. Much of the lower river, especially below the town of Imnaha, is wrapped up in private lands, but a knock on a door can get you permission to fish. Otherwise, watch for Forest Service signs. The last few miles of the river are accessible only by trail.

Upstream from Imnaha, the river continues through lots of private property, but access is good for those willing to ask permission. Above the old sawmill at Pallette Ranch Site (USFS), the river flows entirely through public lands (Wallowa-Whitman National Forest). Above Pallette, you will find six campgrounds along the river, the uppermost being Indian Crossing about a mile from the wilderness boundary. Two other campgrounds are located above the river canyon (Duck Lake and Twin Lakes). The entire 16-mile reach from Indian Crossing down to Pallette offers good fishing, especially between late July and mid-October, when water levels drop and hopper season arrives.

Upstream from Indian Crossing, the Imnaha's wilderness reach begins and while this is a fairly popular trail, serious anglers are in the minority. You can have a pretty good go of it with a fly rod and a pair of wading shoes. A hike of 6.5 miles takes you up to the confluence of the North and South forks and you couldn't possibly cover all the productive pocket water and pool water in the course of a day. The forks themselves offer fair fishing, but the main river is better.

To reach the lower Imnaha and the town of Imnaha, follow Little Sheep Creek Road (Route 350) out of Joseph for some 30 miles. Gravel roads follow the river up- and downstream from Imnaha. If the upper river is your destination, take the scenic Wallowa Mountain Loop Road (Forest Primary Route 39), which turns south off Route 350 about eight miles east of Joseph. The Loop Road crosses Big Sheep Creek after about

Lostine River

Like the Minam River nearby, the beautiful Lostine River offers fair to good fishing for wild trout in an attractive, forested canyon. The Lostine originates at Minam Lake, deep in the Eagle Cap Wilderness, and then flows north for several miles inside the Eagle Cap Wilderness. At the wilderness boundary, the Lostine picks up the East Lostine River and then flows alongside Forest Route 8210. The Lostine, which flows beside several campgrounds along FR8210, is far more heavily fished than the Minam and is also a smaller river. Still, its small trout provide ample entertainment, especially for those who either walk into the wilderness or who ask permission to fish the valley reach between the national forest boundary and the river's confluence with the Wallowa north of the town of Lostine.

Wallowa River

A fair to good stream for wild and planted trout, the Wallowa flows westerly from Wallowa Lake, through the towns of Enterprise, Wallowa and Minam, and then through a deep canyon before joining the Grand Ronde at Rondowa, downstream from Elgin. Good fishing is available from the lake down to Minam, but access is difficult due to private property. Permission is usually granted after a knock on a door. Rainbows from eight to 14 inches abound. Below Minam, the river descends into a fairly inaccessible canyon, which can be floated by experienced white-water boaters. The take-out, however, is on the Grand Ronde, all the way downstream at Wildcat Creek, south of Troy—a two- or three-day float. Guided floats, which include access to some great water, are available through area outfitters. Check with High Country Outfitters at 541/432-9171 or with one of the fishing stores in Joseph.

Imnaha River canyon.

Imnaha River.

20 miles and then winds its way another 15 miles down Gumboot Creek Canyon to the Imnaha a couple miles downstream from Blackhorse Campground.

Minam River

A wilderness river for most of its length, the Minam offers good fishing for native rainbows in a truly beautiful setting. The Minam's headwaters come from Blue Lake and from the flanks of the highest peaks in the Wallowas, deep in the heart of the Eagle Cap Wilderness. From there, the river plunges into a deep, picturesque canyon and flows northwesterly through many miles of wilderness.

The only access other than foot or horseback is a chartered flight into Minam Lodge, situated deep inside the wilderness near the Wallowa/Union County Line. The lodge offers full accommodations and guided river trips, which float all the way down to Troy on the Grand Ronde, via the Minam and Wallowa rivers. The fishing is excellent for wild rainbows and some brown trout. The typical trip consists of a two- or three-day stay at the lodge and then a three-day float trip. For information, contact High Country Outfitters/Minam Lodge at 541/432-9171. Do-it-yourselfers can contact the lodge and put-in there. The drift from Minam Lodge down to the town of Minam covers 22 miles and includes one Class III rapid. The float requires fairly good boating skills as some of the Class II rapids simply go on and on for two or three miles.

The Minam joins the Wallowa River at the little town of Minam, about nine river miles north of the wilderness boundary. Outside the wilderness, the Minam is primarily tied up in private land. A trailhead at the wilderness boundary leads up the Minam on a good trail, but those wishing to reach points deeper in the wilderness can use any of several other trailheads: Consult the Eagle Cap Wilderness Map, available at most Wallowa-Whitman National Forest offices and at many outdoor stores around the state.

Fishing beaver ponds deep in the Blue Mountains.

Wallowa Lake

Ever-popular Wallowa Lake ranks among the must-see sights of northeastern Oregon. This beautiful 1,600-acre lake occupies a narrow glacial basin at the foot of the precipitous Wallowa Mountains just south of the town of Joseph. Popular with kokanee anglers and with splash-and-giggle crowds, the lake does offer some decent summer and fall fishing for 10- to 18-inch rainbows. Mackinaw are present as well, but are no longer stocked. More significantly perhaps, Wallowa Lake serves as a starting point for excursions into the Eagle Cap Wilderness. A nice, though popular campground occupies the shoreline on the south end of the lake.

Eagle Cap Wilderness

At 293,735 acres, the Eagle Cap Wilderness is Oregon's largest designated wilderness area. At its heart are the high peaks of the Wallowa Range, including Matterhorn (9,845 feet), Sacajawea Peak (9,833), Eagle Cap (9,595), Aneroid Mountain (9,702) and numerous others. Included in the wilderness are several productive rivers such as the Minam, upper Lostine and upper Imnaha (see separate listings for each). For the stillwater angler, there are some 75-odd fishable lakes, including many that are rarely visited on account of extreme remoteness.

Brook trout reside in many of the wilderness lakes; rainbows in other and cutthroat in a few. Golden trout were once planted in several of the lakes, but the program was long ago discontinued and, despite an occasional report to the contrary, the goldens have long since died out. The rivers offer wild rainbows along with fully protected bull trout. The northside trailheads—especially the one at Wallowa Lake—are heavily used, but those willing to hike long and hard will find plenty of solitude. The more remote trailheads are lightly used and offer a combination of superb solitude, great scenery and good trout fishing in both lakes and streams.

Be sure to obtain appropriate maps. My collection includes the following, all available from the Wallowa-Whitman National Forest and most available at outdoor stores: Wallowa-Whitman National Forest South Half and North Half; Eagle Cap Wilderness; Eagle Cap Wilderness & Travel Opportunity Guide-Eagle Cap Ranger District; Hells Canyon National Recreation Area.

Wenaha River

A wilderness river and tributary to the Grand Ronde, the Wenaha is a remote and scenic mountain river that flows through a big, forested canyon. All but the lower few miles of the river are encompassed by the 176,800-acre Wenaha-Tucannon Wilderness Area. The Wenaha joins the Grand Ronde at Troy.

The Eagle Cap Wilderness features dozens of productive hike-in lakes.

The North Fork John Day offers a fair run of late-arriving summer steelhead.

Two different fisheries draw attention from fly anglers: Summer steelhead are available during the fall as far upstream as Crooked Creek, although the future of this and other northwestern Oregon steelhead fishing is potentially in doubt due to possible Endangered/Threatened listings. Otherwise, the Wenaha is a trout fishery dominated by wild rainbows. Most are small, but 14- to 16-inch trout are available. By midsummer, when the river runs low and clear, hopper fishing can be exceptional; lots of standard dry flies will work equally well.

The Wenaha has no road access other than right around the mouth of the river in Troy. However, a good trail follows the river for its entire length and a dozen other trails descend to the river from trailheads and Forest Service spur roads all around the perimeter of the wilderness, both on the Oregon side and on the Washington side. The Umatilla National Forest Map will show you the way. Before venturing into the wilderness, check with the Umatilla National Forest for wilderness permits, trail conditions and river conditions (Walla Walla Ranger District: 509/522-6290).

John Day River

Oregon's longest river, the John Day and its major tributaries cut a 275-mile swath through several counties from its headwaters in the Blue Mountains to its confluence with the Columbia about 15 miles east of the Deschutes River. Along its circuitous journey, the John Day offers first-rate fisheries for steelhead, smallmouth bass and trout.

The steelhead begin to arrive at the mouth during late summer, with the bulk of the run entering the river during the fall or winter. Despite some years of impressive harvest statistics, the John Day will never approach the popularity of the Deschutes or Grand Ronde as a steelhead fly-fishing river. Mostly this is because so much of the river is inaccessible due to extensive private lands and because during many seasons the river's warm, low water doesn't spur fish to move upriver until winter or spring. Thus, the harvest numbers can be a bit misleading: Most of the annual harvest comes from trollers working the nine-mile-long pool that fills the lower John Day Canyon. In fact, some of the best fly water on

the river is located immediately above the unfloatable Tumwater Falls at the top end of the canyon pool.

Above the pool, the river flows through remote canyonlands, most of which are private ranch holdings. You should obtain permission to cross these parcels, but obtaining permission can prove a time-consuming task. However, anglers who manage to work out an access to the John Day downstream from the Hwy. 206 crossing can fish some of the river's most productive steelhead water with little chance of seeing another human. Still, approach this concept with the knowledge that you may not find any steelhead until late in the fall or during winter and then venture out with care when the roads get wet. Among the best available maps of the John Day's lower reaches is the BLM's Lower John Day River Public Lands.

The more accessible reach of the river flows from Hwy. 218 at Clarno north to the Cottonwood Access at Hwy. 206. There are public boat accesses at both points, but make sure you know what you are getting into: This is a 70-mile trip that should not be attempted until the flows increase after irrigation season. Straight-through float time might approach 20 hours at low water, so if you plan to spend time looking for steelhead during October or November, plan on a week or so to make the trip and check with the BLM and ODFW before starting out: You will want to know the river flow and color and you'll want some idea of whether any fish are in the river. For those prepared, this can be a memorable float, through some massive canyon country where you won't see many people.

The more significant fishery on the John Day, both in the Clarno to Cottonwood reach and upstream, is provided by abundant smallmouth bass. In fact, the river has gained regional prominence for the quality of its smallmouth fishery. Not only are the bass numerous, but they can reach impressive sizes. Fourteen- to 18-inch fish are not uncommon. Moreover, they will respond to just about all methods, from deep-dredging with weighted nymphs and streamers to shallow-running streamers to dry flies and popping or diving bugs.

Picture Gorge on the John Day River is named for the pictographs on the cliffs.

The John Day River has gained national recognition for its smallmouth bass fishery.

The smallmouth fishing picks up as the water drops to fishable levels during late spring or early summer. During some years, the river drops to a mere trickle by late July, making for difficult boating conditions. However, once the irrigation season ends and a few fall rains refresh the region, floating becomes easy once again.

The next segment upstream from the Clarno to Cottonwood reach begins at Service Creek, on Hwy. 19 west of Spray, and ends at the Clarno take-out. This segment, referred to as the Upper John Day, covers 50 miles. To allow adequate fishing time, plan three or four days for this trip or float it in sections. You can shave 10 miles off the trip by launching at the Twickenham Access, located off Gird's Creek Road: Follow Hwy. 207 north from Mitchell or south from Service Creek and turn northwest on Gird's Creek Road or follow Hwy. 19 southeast from Fossil and turn south from Shelton State Wayside onto Rowe Creek Road. For a one- or two-day trip, float from Service Creek to Twickenham.

Additional put-ins are located still further upstream, one at Spray and one at Kimberly, both allowing for nice one- or two-day floats. Hwy. 19 follows the river through most of this section and then parallels it closely upstream (south) of Kimberly for almost 20 miles to Hwy. 26. Again, this stretch is dominated by private property, but the highway easement provides some access. One can drop a raft into the river at several places between Kimberly and the town of John Day off to the east.

The John Day has become a very popular rafter's river during late spring and early summer: Memorial Day weekend often brings hundreds of floaters to the river, with the stretch from Kimberly to Clarno turning into a parade of sorts. Luckily, the high water of spring that makes the river so attractive to splash-and-gigglers also makes for difficult bass fishing, so smallmouth anglers can wait until the crowds thin before drifting the river.

Upstream from Kimberly, the smallmouth population begins to slowly give way to a trout fishery of marginal quality. Steelhead ascend into this reach as well, but rough fish dominate. From the Hwy. 19/26 junction all the way east to the John Day area, the river is almost completely surrounded by private farm and ranch property. The habitat has suffered accordingly and access is difficult unless you are willing to knock on doors. The steelhead fishery extends upstream to the legal boundary at Indian Creek, between John Day and Prairie City. Generally, steelhead don't arrive in the valley stretch along Hwy. 26 until winter, although in some years, late October and early November fishing can be fair.

The headwaters of the John Day originate in the Blue Mountains near Summit Prairie and some trout fishing is available along the upper 10 miles where the river flows through a patchwork mixture of Forest Service and private land.

North Fork John Day River

Joining the main river at Kimberly, the North Fork John Day travels more than 100 miles from its sources in the Elkhorn Range southwest of La Grande. The North Fork is a marginal trout stream, so its run of late-arriving summer steelhead provides the most prominent fishery. November through March is prime steelhead time, but during some years, severe winter weather can limit the opportunity to a handful of nice days.

Hwy. 395 at Dale, between Mt. Vernon and Pendleton, is the upstream boundary for steelhead fishing. The lower end of the North Fork is accessible from Kimberly-Long Creek Road, which heads northeast from Kimberly and follows the North Fork for almost 15 miles up to Monument. Much of the river flows through private property, so ask permission if you're not sure. Wall Creek Road follows the river for several miles north from Monument and the north end of this dead-end road enters BLM lands for a mile and a half. A 12-mile roadless reach follows and despite quite a bit of BLM land along the river, public access is virtually nil owing to the surrounding private holdings. From Hwy. 395, the upper third of the steelhead water is accessible by road from Dale, although private property still predominates.

The lower end of the North Fork is floatable from Wall Creek to Monument or from either of those two points down to Kimberly. Consult a county map or the Umatilla National Forest map before venturing too far afield in this country.

Middle Fork John Day River

Like the North Fork John Day, the Middle Fork offers fishing for late-arriving summer steelhead. A few fish are taken during late fall, but most fish are caught the following spring as the water begins to warm. Some wild rainbows are available, but the trout fishery has generally been dominated by hatchery plants. The Middle Fork flows through lots of private land downstream from Hwy. 395 (the upstream steelhead fishing boundary),

Lower John Day River.

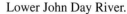
FRANK AMATO PHOTO

FRANK AMATO PHOTO

Gail McDougal on North Fork John Day with summer-run steelhead.

but permission can be secured with a knock on a door or two (although finding the right door can present a problem in places).

Hwy. 395 crosses the Middle Fork about halfway between the wide spot of Dale and the tiny village of Long Creek. Just north of the highway bridge, the road down to Ritter takes off to the west, providing access to all but the lower ten miles of the river, which flow through a roadless expanse of private ranch holdings. In the heart of this remote roadless reach, the Middle Fork joins the North Fork John Day.

Umatilla River

The Umatilla River offers a small, but often productive run of summer steelhead that arrive in the fall, after precipitation cools and raises the water in this small stream. Several hundred hatchery fish are tagged each year. The best fly water extends from the town of Pendleton downstream to Echo, along Old Pendleton River Road, which is accessed from the west end of Pendleton (freeway Exit 207).

This entire reach lies to the south of Interstate 84 and most of it flows through private lands. Be sure to seek permission before fishing. The river offers many classic fly runs. During late fall, when the best fly fishing occurs, chukars can be heard calling from the rimrocks and an occasional pheasant will dash across the road or explode from riverside cover.

Above Pendleton, the river flows through the Umatilla Indian Reservation, where fishing is prohibited except by permit on waters open by the tribal fish and wildlife agency. At least half of the river's headwaters, however, are preserved in the North Fork Umatilla Wilderness on the west slope of the Blue Mountains almost due east of Pendleton. The wilderness waters offer productive small-stream fishing for wild rainbows. Bull trout, which also inhabit the system, are afforded full protection. These headwater areas are restricted to catch-and-release fishing with artificial flies and lures.

The North Fork Umatilla Wilderness is most easily accessible from trailheads located just south or west of Hwy. 204, the Weston-Elgin Road. Other approaches are from Forest Service spur roads leading in from the south. The Umatilla National Forest Map details the area.

Canyon Creek Meadows Reservoir (Canyon Meadows Lake)

During years of good water supply, 35-acre Canyon Creek Meadows Reservoir (often called Canyon Creek Lake) near John Day can produce planted rainbows to 16 inches along with some decent-sized brook trout and a few cutthroat, the latter two species being wild. Best fishing occurs early, but check with ODFW before trying to access the reservoir (elevation 5,045 feet) in the spring. Typically, the reservoir freezes in December and thaws by late March or early April.

After being filled for the first time in 1964, the Canyon Meadows Lake immediately began to leak and now goes virtually dry almost every

summer, so the fishing generally ends by mid- to late July. Nonetheless, the lake sits in a nice setting and provides good early season float-tube action even though the trout don't have much chance to grow. During very wet years, which don't occur often, fishing can hold up through the season.

A good ramp provides boat access (no motors allowed), but a float tube is perfect for this small reservoir. A Forest Service campground is situated amidst ponderosas adjacent to the lake. Follow Hwy. 395 south out of John Day for about 10 miles and turn southeast on Canyon Creek Road (County Road 65/Forest Road 15). Follow Canyon Creek Road another 10 miles or so to FR1520 and turn left to reach the reservoir.

Pilcher Creek Reservoir

A productive rainbow reservoir located west of North Powder (south of La Grande), Pilcher Creek offers good fishing during May and June for rainbows that can reach 18 inches and tend to average 10 to 14 inches. Follow the road to Anthony Lakes west out of North Powder (Exit 285 off I-84), then after about three miles, continue due west up to Forest Road 4330, which accesses the 125-acre reservoir. The west side of the reservoir features shallow shoals perfect for fly fishing from a float tube or pontoon boat. Chironomid hatches produce rises during morning and evenings, although the strength and intensity of the emergences vary considerably. *Callibaetis* mayflies appear during May and June.

Wolf Creek Reservoir

Located a few miles west of North Powder (south of La Grande), 200-acre Wolf Creek Reservoir offers fair to good float-tube fishing between April and June most years. Heavy irrigation draw reduces the pool substantially by fall, so few trout have a chance to grow large. Nonetheless, fishing for 10- to 14-inch fish can be excellent at times, mostly on the north arm of the lake in the area around the inlet. Follow I-84 to exit 283 (north of North Powder) and follow Wolf Creek Road west a few miles to the reservoir.

The Umatilla River, pictured here below Pendleton, offers a fair to good run of summer steelhead.

WILLAMETTE ZONE

Oregon's temperate Willamette Valley, stretching from Portland on the north to the Eugene area on the south, is home to most of the state's three-million-plus residents. It was this fertile valley, in fact, that beckoned the first white settlers to the Northwest, although native peoples had occupied the land for thousands of years.

Today's Willamette Valley is a hustle-and-bustle world in many respects, with Interstate-5 cutting a north-south path through the heart of the valley, connecting the busy cities of Portland, Salem and Eugene along with the smaller cities in between. Yet despite the mass of people who live and work in this lush, hundred-mile-long valley, outdoor enthusiasts have no trouble finding ways to satisfy their wants and fly anglers are no exception.

The Willamette River itself offers a variety of options, including productive trout waters in its upstream reaches. Nearby, the famed McKenzie River offers some of the state's best dry-fly angling. Most of the large tributaries to the Willamette offer runs of hatchery and in some cases wild summer steelhead; Native winter steelhead, their numbers much reduced, still ascend the Willamette and its tributaries and the wild runs are augmented in some streams by hatchery plants. Among the steelhead streams are regional favorites such as the North Santiam, South Santiam, McKenzie and Clackamas.

Historically, the Willamette Valley was one giant flood plain that was inundated each winter and spring by heavy rains and run-off from the Cascades and Coast Range. Flood-control dams on all the major rivers eventually stabilized the flood plain, allowing towns to arise in areas once uninhabitable and allowing farmers to pioneer new agricultural lands. Prior to the installation of the dams, the great winter and spring floods allowed anadromous fish easy passage over Willamette Falls (at Oregon City near Portland). But during dry summers, when the river shrank to a fraction of its rainy-season mass, anadromous fish could not negotiate the falls. Only with the installation of a fish ladder and the planting of hatchery summer steelhead have rivers such as the North Santiam become good fly-rod steelhead rivers.

By virtue of its borders, the ODFW's Willamette Zone encompasses a wide array of fisheries, from the valley rivers previously mentioned to countless small mountain lakes, many of which are inside several large wilderness areas. Anglers who want to get away from the crowds and fish productive lakes for brook trout, rainbow and cutthroat should peruse maps of the Mt. Jefferson Wilderness and the Three Sisters Wilderness.

Dave Hughes with Willamette River cutthroat trout.

JIM SCHOLLMEYER PHOTO

McKenzie River

The Willamette River's most renowned trout stream, the McKenzie River has for decades been a favorite haunt of local anglers and an important destination for fly fisher's visiting from other states. This bold, beautiful river offers just about everything one could hope for in a western Oregon trout stream: Its lower reaches offer large wild rainbows and cutthroat, its middle section features splendid scenery and challenging water for the drift-boater and its upper end harbors small wild trout in an equally wild setting characterized by deep, bubble-shot plunge pools and breathtakingly cold, clear waters.

The McKenzie begins its journey at Clear Lake in the Cascade Mountains. The lake is aptly named, for its vibrant depths attract the attention of scuba divers who marvel at the incredible clarity. Below Clear Lake, the river gouges a narrow passage through ancient bedrock; its boulder- and ledge-studded path replete with extravagantly green ferns and mosses and shaded by dense conifers. Just below the lake, the McKenzie crosses under Hwy. 126 and plunges over Sahalie Falls in a shroud of dampening mist and then over the sheer, roaring drop at Koosah Falls.

This small but treacherous reach of the McKenzie is followed by trails on both banks between Sahalie Falls and Carmen Reservoir a mile or so below. Despite its proximity to the highway, this upper end of the river is not heavily fished and is best enjoyed by those with a fair degree of athleticism. Its small wild rainbows and brook trout are a treat and an occasional rare bull trout must be carefully released.

The Upper McKenzie is first impounded at Carmen Diversion Reservoir, itself offering good float-tube angling for small wild brook trout and stocked rainbows that occasionally reach 18 inches. At Carmen Reservoir, however, the river is diverted and fishing doesn't resume until you reach the canyon section above Trail Bridge Reservoir.

Below Trail Bridge Reservoir, the McKenzie gains size and strength. Between Trail Bridge and Leaburg Dam, the McKenzie offers many different put-ins and take-outs, so anglers interested in working the upper river can choose a drift that fits their time constraints. The uppermost ramp is located well upriver at Olallie Creek Campground and another is located a few miles below at Frissell Creek. The next ramp is located at Paradise Campground, two miles downriver from the junction of Hwy. 126 and Hwy. 242 (Old McKenzie Highway). About four miles further downstream is the launch at McKenzie Bridge Campground. A dozen more launches are located between McKenzie Bridge and Leaburg Dam.

The entire upper river (Olallie to Leaburg) features exciting but easy water with one exception: the Class IV Marten Rapids, located downstream from Ben & Kay Dorris State Park. Bank access is good on most of the river above Leaburg, where the most prominent catch will be hatchery-reared, put-and-take rainbows, which are fin-clipped to help anglers identify the river's wild redside rainbows and cutthroat trout, which must be released unharmed.

Below Leaburg, bank access is a problem owing to extensive private property, so the McKenzie becomes the domain of drift boats. Several of the launch areas provide access to the banks and these areas include some of the river's top runs and pools for summer steelhead. The steelhead arrive between June and September, with peak fishing from July into the fall. These are the same hatchery-reared Skamania-strain fish that also return to the North and South Santiam, Willamette, Molalla and Clackamas rivers. During a good year, the McKenzie's run will total between 2,000 and 5,000 fish.

The McKenzie, like the other Willamette Valley steelhead streams, seems almost tailor-made for classic dry-line techniques. The same flies that have served me so well on the North Santiam—namely Forrest Maxwell's Purple Matuka and my Spawning Purple—have enjoyed consistent success on the McKenzie. Other classics will prove equally effective, including patterns such as the Skunk, Green-Butt Skunk, Silver Hilton and Purple Peril.

From the first put-in below Leaburg Dam (Greenwood Road Access) to Hendrick's Park east of Springfield, hatchery rainbow trout predominate (after all, the river is stocked with well over 100,000 of these fish). However, as you progress down river, wild rainbows and cutthroat become more prevalent and hatchery fish are not stocked below Hayden Bridge in Springfield. The river below Leaburg is a favorite stretch for many anglers

Above Leaburg, the McKenzie features mostly planted rainbows.

because the trout are plentiful and the hatches strong. The entire stretch from Leaburg Dam down to the river's mouth is open year round.

From Hendrick's Park down to the mouth of the river north of Eugene, the McKenzie offers its most intriguing fishery. This stretch is dominated by wild trout and managed for their protection. Only artificial flies and lures are allowed and, as with the rest of the river, wild trout must be released. Below Hayden Bridge, hatchery trout are uncommon and the wild trout, along with abundant whitefish, provide the action. McKenzie River redbands can reach 20 inches in this reach; cutthroat top out at about 16 inches, although an occasional lunker shows up.

The lower river meanders at a gentle gradient, creating ideal habitat for trout to grow large on abundant insects, including some exceptional hatches. Wide, shallow gravel and cobblestone bars predominate and during strong hatches the large wild trout line up along the near-shore shallows and rise freely.

The big fish—even many of the small trout—can feed with a degree of selectivity usually reserved for spring creek trout. The McKenzie is heavily fished and the trout learn quickly the value of careful, selective feeding. Anglers wishing to hook the big fish should learn the value of a quiet approach and a delicate presentation.

The season begins with the highly anticipated hatch of Western March brown mayflies (*Rhithrogena morrisoni*), whose emergence often begins on warm, February afternoons. March and April offer the best March brown hatches. These elegant mayflies are imitated with size 12 and 14 hooks. A tan Sparkle Dun or Compara-Dun usually does the trick; if not, try an emerger pattern fished in the film or just under the surface. The March Brown Soft-hackle, tied in a variety of dressings by different anglers over the years, is one such pattern.

Blue-winged olives (*Baetis*) emerge during winter and spring when water levels cooperate. The hatches generally occur during the afternoon, especially on muggy, still days during winter and warm, cloudy days during spring. Also among the early hatches are little black stoneflies

The beautiful uppermost reaches of the McKenzie offer plunge-pool fishing for the physically oriented.

and early black stoneflies. The latter is a fairly large insect, smoky brown on the back, pale yellowish brown on the bottom. Size 6 through 10 hooks imitate them. Neither of these stoneflies hatch in big numbers, but both can bring trout to the surface on warm days during periods when the water drops to good fishing levels.

Early season fishing on the McKenzie is in fact quite dependent on river levels. Heavy rains in the region can swell the river to unruly proportions, making it unfishable for days, even weeks, on end. On occasion an entire winter and early spring will pass with only a few fishable days. During drier years, the lower river drops into shape after each rainstorm.

The March brown and blue-winged olive hatches last through the spring, even into June some years. By May, however, another insect of equal significance joins the hatch parade, the famed McKenzie caddis (*Arctopsyche grandis*). Evening emergences of these large green caddisflies can trigger extensive rises up and down the river, drawing the river's largest trout into the shallows where the majority of the insects hatch. The adult McKenzie caddis is imitated with size 8 and 10 hooks. The insect's body is a bright green, almost iridescent in certain light conditions, and the wings are dark gray. The classic dry pattern, called the McKenzie Green Caddis, varies slightly in interpretation, but is essentially dressed as follows:

McKenzie Green Caddis

Hook: Dry fly, size 8-10
Tail: Natural deer hair
Body: Bright peacock-green yarn or dubbing
Hackle: Grizzly, palmered through body
Wing: Natural gray deer hair
Collar: Grizzly hackle

Recent versions of this old McKenzie River standby sometimes feature a body of peacock herl or wings of partridge tied spent style. During the hatch, however, pupa patterns often outfish the adult imitation. For the dry-fly enthusiast, this isn't necessarily bad news because a large green-bodied X-Caddis fishes quite well. Otherwise, try an Antron Caddis Pupa or LaFontaine Caddis Pupa.

Other caddis are both widespread and abundant and I can't claim to have done a thing to further the cause of keying out the different McKenzie caddis genera and species. Nor have I found any need to do so. A selection of X-Caddis and spent caddis patterns, ranging in size from 12 through 18 always seems more than a match for the myriad caddis hatches that occur during the summer.

A new batch of mayflies arrives by June and July, including a vibrant, bright yellow member of the *Epeorus* clan whose size 12-14 adults are truly among the most beautiful mayflies I have ever seen. Unfortunately, these elegant insects never hatch en masse and the trout seem barely to notice the scattered individuals. The same insect occurs regularly on the North Santiam and several other Willamette Valley streams.

Among the river's most unheralded hatches is the June emergence of green drakes, whose arrival is a fleeting affair lasting from three to ten days or so. The insects hatch in earnest only on cloudy days around mid-June and entire seasons can go by without a strong hatch, although the typical year will offer several days running during which the hatch comes off strong at midday. Pale morning duns (*Ephemerella*) are common as well and they too hatch best on cloudy days during May and June and during the morning and/or evening during July. An occasional hatch of pale evening duns (*Heptagenia*) occurs as well, typically between mid- and late summer. Both the PMDs and the *Heptagenia*'s can be easily imitated with a pale olive-tan Sparkle Dun.

By autumn, a few small caddis linger, including a tiny black caddis that, when present in numbers, can bring rising fish to the shorelines in the lower river. Blue-winged olives hatch from time to time as well, but the October caddis can steal the show if they should happen to arrive en masse. These are the big, orange *Dicosmoecus* caddis common to several other Oregon trout streams. I spent many an autumn Saturday standing in the riffle below Armitage Park listening to the uproarious crowd at Autzen stadium and wondering what I was missing; likewise, I've spent a few sunny October Saturdays in Autzen Stadium, wishing by the third quarter that I was over at Armitage Park.

Access to the lower end of the McKenzie is available from several locations: Armitage Park just north of Eugene, from which you can walk up and down river for a fair distance, is the most popular access. A take-out is located at the park. McKenzie View Drive, which follows the north bank east of I5, offers fair access in places, although you will have to seek permission to cross the private lands in many locales. Other Springfield-area accesses are available at and around Hayden Bridge and a little further downriver at Harvest Lane. Camp Creek Road provides access to a few stretches on the north bank above Hayden Bridge, including Bellinger Landing, which is a good launch site for a float down to Armitage. The Harvest Lane access includes a ramp, as does the Hayden Bridge Access. Four additional ramps are located between Greenwood Road Access (below Leaburg) and Springfield. You can also float down past Armitage and fish the mouth of the McKenzie and the adjacent Willamette, taking out at Hileman Landing of Beacon Road north of Santa Clara.

John Shewey covers a steelhead run on the McKenzie below Leaburg.

Willamette River (mainstem).

JIM SCHOLLMEYER PHOTO

Willamette River (mainstem)

Lifeblood of the fertile Willamette Valley, the Willamette River offers several distinct reaches of interest to fly anglers. Among the most popular is the section of river passing through Eugene and Santa Clara at the valley's south end. Native cutthroat and rainbow inhabit this section and some of the rainbows reach 20 inches. What's more, this unlikely stretch of water features a preponderance of excellent hatches, including the McKenzie Caddis, a large, green-bodied caddis well known from the nearby and more famous McKenzie River.

Other significant hatches include Western March brown mayflies, which emerge during the spring, blue-winged olives (*Baetis*), and brown willow flies (a variety of golden stonefly) that hatch sporadically between mid-spring and late summer. Even *Tricorythodes* (Trico) mayflies occur in dense swarms on parts of the Willamette. Better known on famous spring creeks, such as the Henry's Fork in Idaho, these "tiny white-winged blacks" appear on late-summer mornings—a time of year when few fly anglers venture to the Willamette below Eugene.

Even right through the city, the Willamette offers good fly angling when water levels cooperate between early spring and mid-autumn. The reach directly behind Valley River Center (a large shopping mall) has long been a favorite of local anglers. Nearly as productive is the reach upstream from the University of Oregon, above the I5 Bridge.

A drift boat will provide access to lightly fished sections of the river. Launches are located at Alton Baker Park in Eugene and in Santa Clara off River Road (Whitely Landing and Hileman Landing). Seven additional launches are located between Santa Clara and Corvallis. In addition to the aforementioned reaches in Eugene, the two launches in Santa Clara offer bank access to some productive water. The Willamette can also be negotiated by jet-sled for those who want to run up or down to a favorite riffle.

Middle Fork Willamette

A good rainbow stream with artificials-only, catch-and-release regulations in effect year round, the Middle Fork Willamette above Lookout Point Reservoir is a regional favorite for anglers from the southern Willamette Valley. Rainbows here run ten to 14 inches, with trout to 20 inches available. During low flows, good hatches of caddis, stoneflies and mayflies prompt good surface action.

Some productive stretches of the river are easily accessible off Hwy. 58, which follows the Middle Fork from Dexter Dam to Oakridge. Check the Willamette National Forest map and county maps to learn the north bank roads. The best reach is from Oakridge down to Dexter Reservoir. The section above Hills Creek Reservoir also produces some good fish and the tailwater reach below Dexter Dam offers the added bonus of summer steelhead from June through early autumn. This lower section is floatable: The uppermost launches are below Dexter Dam (both banks) and a few miles below at the Pengra Access three miles west of Lowell on Pengra Road (on the north bank). Down-river ramps are located about five miles downstream at Jasper Bridge and two miles further, off Clearwater Lane in Springfield (Clearwater Landing).

Dewey Weddington fishes a side-channel on the Willamette River near Santa Clara.

Gold Lake

One of Oregon's precious few fly-fishing-only lakes, Gold Lake offers good fishing for rainbows averaging 12 to 14 inches and reaching 20 inches, along with brook trout from six to 16 inches. This 100-acre lake is ideally suited to float tubes, pontoon boats, canoes and other small craft. The lake is situated in the Cascades, southeast of Eugene, just off Hwy. 58 near Willamette Pass.

Owing to catch-and-release regulations on the rainbows, Gold Lake remains productive year in and year out. The only problem may be the self-sustaining brook trout, which have multiplied so rapidly that ODFW encourages anglers to keep as many as they want with no restrictions on size or number. Each year the brook trout seem to increase in numbers while decreasing in average size. Their success no doubt comes at the expense of the rainbows, whose presence, average size, and propensity for eating dry flies during the mayfly hatch have traditionally attracted fly anglers to this attractive Cascades lake.

Indeed, the *Callibaetis* mayfly hatch is Gold Lake's biggest draw. The mayflies, called speckled-wing duns, emerge all summer and into early fall, providing reliable and frequently exciting surface action. your best bet is the far side of the lake (the northeast end) where shallow, weedy shoals offer ideal mayfly habitat that is frequented by the lake's rainbows.

Gold Lake is accessed from Hwy. 58, which traverses the Cascades between Eugene and Central Oregon's Hwy. 97. Follow Hwy. 58 east from Oakridge or west from Hwy. 97. Just west of Willamette Pass, Forest Road 500 turns sharply to the north and leads about two miles up to the lake. The road, which is signed at the highway, is usually open by early or mid-June. A campground occupies the south shoreline and a 1/2-mile trail leads down to Upper and Lower Marilyn lakes, both good for smallish brook trout.

Lost Lake (Santiam Pass)

Located immediately adjacent to Hwy. 22, just west of Santiam Pass summit, Lost Lake offers easy-access float-tube fishing for brook trout, rainbows and Atlantic salmon. The lake covers about 80 acres and is shallow throughout. By late summer, Lost Lake often shrinks to little more than a vast marsh with a few open-water potholes where fish seek refuge.

During years of good water supply, when the fish over-summer and survive the winter, Lost Lake produces fish to 18 inches, sometimes larger. All three species grow quite rapidly in the lake's fertile, weedy waters. In years past, a chance at 16- to 20-inch brook trout was the big draw at Lost Lake, but following several dry years in the late 80s/early 90s and following the introduction of the other species, the population of big brook trout has not yet returned to form. However, an occasional big brookie still makes an appearance and the rainbows sometimes reach 18 inches as well.

Lost Lake is an artificials-only, catch-and-release water, so the fishery remains productive despite the hordes of worm-drowners who no doubt stare longingly from the highway that runs along the south shore. Trout and salmon ten to 14 inches abound and an occasional Lost Lake brook trout of 18 inches is a chunky, colorful beast that makes the trip well worthwhile.

Callibaetis mayflies begin emerging by early summer and continue into September. Good dry-fly fishing is the rule once the hatch gets underway. Caddis and midge emergences create plenty of surface action as well. By mid- to late June, a little-known hatch of giant traveling sedges erupts just after dark. The big olive sedges skitter about on the surface laying their eggs and trout abandon all caution in the dark of night to pursue the insects. In order to enjoy this hatch you must push the regulations to their limit: The hatch doesn't even begin until well after sunset, about the same time that legal fishing hours draw to a close (night fishing for trout is not allowed in Oregon).

Damsels hatch each day during midsummer. Fish a nymph near the reed stands or willows between 9 a.m. and noon. All the other typical stillwater trout foods are well represented in Lost Lake. During non-hatch periods, try Woolly Buggers, Zug Bugs, soft-hackle patterns or any of numerous other attractor-type flies.

Highways 126, 20 and 22 converge two miles west of Lost Lake, providing access from the Willamette Valley. From Central Oregon, follow Hwy. 20 west through Sisters and over Santiam Pass to the lake. A gravel road dumps off the highway at the southwest corner of the lake, providing access to myriad campsites along the west shore. Shoreline fishing is possible in places, but this lake is perfectly suited to float tubes and the like.

Lost Lake (Mt. Hood National Forest)

Giant *Hexagenia* mayflies provide the excitement at beautiful and popular Lost Lake in the Mt. Hood National Forest. These giant yellow mayflies begin their nightly emergence after July 4 and continue in strength for two or three weeks, tapering off after that. You can usually count on good hatches during the middle of July. Lost Lake's brown, rainbow and brook trout crash the surface in a frenzy trying to capture the enormous insects (two inches long, tails included). Brown trout can run to 20 inches; 12- to 16-inch specimens are more typical. Same goes for the rainbows.

Most of the action occurs on the west side of the lake, where shallow, mud-bottom shoals provide ideal habitat for the borrowing *Hexagenia limbata* nymphs. The nymphs begin to emerge from their burrows around sunset and the best action generally occurs at dusk on cool days or after dark on hot days. Opinions vary as to the best fly patterns, but yellow extended-body para-drakes are consistent producers. The bodies on these flies should be tied about an inch long, even a little more. Down-wing "cripple" patterns also fish well.

Motorboats are not allowed on Lost Lake and the lake is large enough that float-tubers will want to pack their tubes by trail around the north end to reach the shoals on the west side. The hike covers less than a mile. The lodge, located on the northeast side of the lake, offers supplies and rental boats.

South Santiam River.

JIM SCHOLLMEYER PHOTO

Ted Groszkiewikz on the North Santiam River.

While the *Hexagenia* hatch is the big draw for fly anglers, Lost Lake also offers a good *Callibaetis* hatch throughout the summer and some decent caddis activity. Autumn fishing can be very good with streamers and attractor patterns.

Easiest access to Lost Lake is from the town of Hood River. Follow Hwy. 35 up the hill and out of town, then follow the signs to Dee and then to Lost Lake via Forest Primary Route 13. From the south, follow Hwy. 26 to Zigzag, then turn north up the Sandy River on FR18, which winds its way over Lolo Pass and then down to FR13 a few miles east of the lake.

Mill Creek (Yamhill River system)

A pleasant little trout stream in its upper reaches, Mill Creek drains the east slope of the Coast Range about 25 miles west of Salem. Small native cutthroat and wild rainbows are abundant, with an average fish spanning perhaps eight inches. However, the deeper pools that lie hidden from the road often harbor fish in the 10- to 14-inch range. Access is from Mill Creek Road, which turns south off Hwy. 22 at Buell, a few miles east of the Hwy. 22/Hwy. 18 junction.

South Santiam River

The South Santiam yields good numbers of steelhead during years when the Willamette system's summer run is strong. Most of these fish, however, are taken by plunkers in the mile of river right below Foster Dam. On crowded weekends during the summer, expect a zoo comparable to those of the coastal chinook stream in the fall. Under such conditions, fly anglers can do one of two things: Pull up a chair and offer round-by-round scoring of any fist-fights that break out, or seek some of the nice fly water to be found further downstream.

The upper South Santiam (above Green Peter Reservoir) flows for about 20 miles from its headwater creeks in the Cascades west of Santiam Pass. Highway 20 follows closely the entire length, allowing good access for trout anglers. Legal-size hatchery rainbows abound during summer and a few wild cutthroat and rainbows are mixed in as well. Many of the tributary creeks of the South Santiam offer good fly angling for small wild trout. A copy of the Willamette National Forest Map will get you started in the right direction.

North Santiam River

During years when the Willamette River's run of hatchery summer steelhead is strong, the North Santiam offers fair to good fly angling for these five- to 15-pound fish. The North Santiam flows west out of the Cascades, through two reservoirs, and eventually into the Willamette south of Salem.

The best stretch for steelhead extends from Stayton up to Big Cliff Dam, with the Mehama to Packsaddle Park being the most popular segment therein. Hwy. 22 follows the river along this stretch and several parks and campgrounds offer good access to the river. These include Fisherman's Bend Campground one mile west of Mill City, North Santiam Park a few miles downriver from Fisherman's Bend and Neale Park on the south bank in Lyons. There are boat launches at all these places; other launches are at Mill City and further upstream at Packsaddle Park. Only experienced boaters should negotiate the river.

It was on the North Santiam that noted steelhead angler Forrest Maxwell devised his Purple Matuka and this fly remains one of the river's most popular and productive steelhead patterns. Other popular choices include the following: Purple Peril, Green Butt Skunk, Spawning Purple, Skunk and Silver Hilton. Over the years since the hatchery summer steelhead fishery was first implemented in the Willamette tributaries, several other effective patterns have been devised by the region's dedicated steelhead anglers.

Fly fishing begins when sufficient numbers of fish have crossed Willamette Falls (fish counts are listed in the Salem *Statesman Journal* and other area newspapers) and when the water drops to fishable levels (fly anglers like to see river-level readings of 2.8 to 3.4 feet). During most years, these two scenarios come about early to mid-June. Fishing lasts until mid-September, when water releases begin at the reservoirs upstream.

To reach the North Santiam, follow Highway 22 east from the I5/Hwy. 22 interchange in Salem. The drive to Mill City covers about 35 miles. Camping is available at Neale Park and Fisherman's Bend.

Willamette Valley Steelhead Patterns

Maxwell's Purple Matuka (Forrest Maxwell)

Tag:	Flat silver tinsel
Body:	Black dubbing (seal's fur or similar)
Rib:	Medium or wide oval silver
Wing:	Four purple hackles (neck hackles)
Collar:	Purple hackle
Variations:	Silver tinsel body or gold tinsel body

Spawning Purple (John Shewey)

Tag/underbody:	Flat silver tinsel
Body:	Fluorescent fire orange flat-waxed nylon thread
Wing:	Five separate "spikes" of purple marabou
Hackle:	Purple
Cheeks:	Jungle cock
Collar:	Guinea, dyed hot orange

Green-Butt Hilton Spider (Dave McNeese)

Tag:	Silver flat tinsel
Tail:	Pintail or teal flank
Butt:	Fluorescent green dubbing
Body:	Black dubbing
Rib:	Medium or wide silver oval
Wings:	Grizzly hackles, tied back and splaying outwards over the body
Collar:	Pintail or teal flank

North Santiam, Upper

Above the town of Detroit, along Hwy. 22, the North Santiam enters Detroit Reservoir. Although crowded during summer, the reach where the river and reservoir (below Blowout Bridge) converge can produce good fall fishing for hatchery-produced rainbows and a few kokanee. Both average nine to 12 inches, but a few trout to 16 inches are available. Same story for the mouths of several other creeks that feed the reservoir, including French Creek, accessed by driving across Detroit Dam.

Above Detroit Reservoir, the river flows alongside Hwy. 22 for 25-odd miles and offers easy-access fishing for planted legal-size rainbows. About 10 miles above the little village of Marion Forks, the highway crosses the river and from here the remaining eight miles of the North Santiam is accessed primarily by trail. The river originates at Santiam Lake, inside the Mt. Jefferson Wilderness Area. A few miles of river are accessible from the Big Meadows area: Just south (uphill) of the highway bridge, turn east on Big Meadows Road, drive about a mile and veer left to reach Big Meadows Campground. The campground road crosses the river, but access is almost entirely by hiking the horse trail along the river and by bushwhacking above and below the campground. Or, instead of veering left to the campground, drive another two miles to Duffy Lake Trailhead. The trail into the wilderness picks up the river after about a mile.

From the highway bridge up to Santiam Lake, the river contains small native cutthroat with brook trout becoming increasingly common as you move closer to the lake. The brook trout, residualized in the stream, are downstream escapees from Toms Lake and Santiam Lake. A 10-inch specimen would qualify as a lunker, but you'll have most of the stream to yourself.

Abiqua Creek

A small stream draining the foothills east of Salem, Abiqua Creek contains native cutthroat and wild rainbows, both of which average about eight inches. Best fishing and best access is on the mainstem above Abiqua Falls. The stream is lightly fished due to extensive private property, but above the falls it offers small-stream fishing in a quiet setting with little company.

Breitenbush River

A heavily fished tributary to Detroit Reservoir east of Salem, the Breitenbush River is mostly a put-and-take fishery for hatchery rainbows, although its more remote upper waters contain small native cutthroat trout. The river runs cold and clear through the Breitenbush Canyon, entirely within public lands, so summer brings crowds.

Silver Creek

Fishing Silver Creek State Park is interesting not so much for the native cutthroat, which max out at about 10 inches, but for the exquisite scenery derived from the series of spectacular waterfalls that make the area a favorite for local sightseers. To reach Silver Creek, follow Hwy. 22 east out of Salem some ten miles to the Silver Creek Falls Exit. Then just follow the signs for the next 15 miles until you arrive at the park. Summer weekends are always crowded—not with anglers, but with waterfall gazers.

This Santiam River summer steelhead was taken during the peak of the run in July.

Round Lake in the Cascades.

JIM SCHOLLMEYER PHOTO

Marion Lake

Three-hundred-sixty-acre Marion Lake is the most popular of the 65-odd fishable lakes in the Mt. Jefferson Wilderness. The lake contains native cutthroat along with naturally reproducing brook trout and rainbows. Rainbow trout are stocked as well and the brookies and rainbows predominate in the catch.

With depths reaching 180 feet and lots of near-shore shallows, Marion Lake is capable of producing rainbows to about 20 inches and brook trout almost that size. Rainbows of ten to 14 inches are common. Insect life is rather abundant for a Cascade Mountains lake. A strong *Callibaetis* mayfly hatch (speckled-wing duns) begins in June and lasts through the summer. Chironomid hatches dominate in the evenings, although as dusk arrives be on the lookout for giant traveling sedges: inch-long olive caddis that skitter across the surface to lay their eggs, throwing the trout into a feeding frenzy.

The hike into Marion Lake covers about 2.5 miles, but another one to two miles, depending on which way you go, takes you to the less-crowded back side of the lake. To reach the trailhead, follow Hwy. 22 east out of Salem about 70 miles to the tiny town of Marion Forks. Turn onto Marion Creek Road (across from the restaurant) and drive to the end, where a large parking area is located. Ice-out generally occurs during April, but the trails may not be snow-free until some time in June.

Round Lake

Located near the headwaters of the Collowash River on the southern edge of the Mt. Hood National Forest, Round Lake offers a reproducing population of brown, brook and rainbow trout. This is a walk-in fly/artificial lure-only lake. The trail covers about half a mile. Brown trout to 20 inches or more are occasionally taken, though average specimens run a foot or so in length. A float tube is a good idea as shoreline fishing is limited around this nine-acre lake.

To find Round Lake, follow Clackamas River Road past Ripplebrook to Collowash River Road (FR63), which crosses the upper Clackamas and then continues south along the Collowash. Stay on 63, which will eventually split into FR6380 and 6370. Follow FR6370 about six miles further until you reach the parking area/trailhead. The short trail is on the east side of the road. You can get there from the south (e.g. Salem/Eugene/Bend) by following Breitenbush Road out of Detroit up to Humbug Road (4696), then following Humbug Road on three miles of pavement, then gravel, past a right turn at FR4698. After passing 4698, follow a lengthy gravel road up the creek until you come to a fork near the creek's headwaters. Stay to the right and wind your way up a heavily clear-cut ridge until you top out at another major intersection and see a sign announcing Mt. Hood National Forest. Turn left (north) on FR6370 and drive about six miles down to the parking area.

Clackamas River

For gear anglers, the Clackamas River is one of the most significant of the Willamette Zone streams. It is heavily fished for summer steelhead, winter steelhead and chinook salmon. Until recently, the Clackamas offered a fine run of summer steelhead in the great fly water of the upper river, but concerns over native anadromous species caused ODFW to discontinue stocking steelhead in the upper river.

Should the stocking program ever resume, the upper river, within the national forest, offers countless exquisite runs, pools and tailouts where traditionalists can deliver a long line and fish classic wet flies or skated dry flies. The upper river is also far more accessible for bank angling than is the lower river. Clackamas River Highway (Oregon Route 224) parallels the river all the way to its headwater sources. Along the way are numerous campgrounds. Like the other Willamette Valley steelhead streams, the upper Clackamas is an easy read, so to speak: Its well-defined pools and runs are recognizable as good steelhead water even to a marginally practiced eye.

The Upper Clackamas offers miles of easily accessible steelhead water.

The Lower Clackamas near Estacada.

water at and below the park. To reach McIver from Estacada, turn right on Hwy. 211 (toward Molalla) and cross the river. After three-quarters of a mile, turn right on Hayden Road and right again on Springwater Road. Follow Springwater Road a mile or so north to the park.

A popular take-out and launch for lower-river drifts, Barton Park is located about eight river miles below Estacada. About six miles below Barton Park is the Carver Ramp, located on the south bank just across the bridge. You can see the ramp just upstream as you cross the bridge and the turn-in is located a couple hundred yards east from Rock Garden Tavern, off Springwater Road. A final take-out is located in Clackamas at Riverside Park near the ODFW district office on Evelyn Road, but I'd suggest leaving this lower end of the river to the plunkers.

Winter steelhead provide another opportunity for fly anglers, but you'll have to bide your time looking for periods of dropping water and you will generally be competing for space with hardware anglers. Eagle Creek, an important tributary of the Clackamas, is another stream worth exploring during the January through March time frame.

Eagle Creek (Clackamas Tributary)

A productive stream for winter steelhead between December and March, Eagle Creek is a favorite haunt of many Portland-based gear fishermen. The stream offers some good fly water, but finding room to operate is frequently a problem: Eagle Creek is simply too close to Portland. Extreme low-water conditions during winter will scare off a few of the jig-and-bobber anglers and a few of the other hardware tossers, but even

Summer-run steelhead.

The upper Clackamas offers stunning landscapes as well, flowing through a deep, forested canyon whose steep sides are studded in places with sheer rock escarpments. The good fly water begins just above the back-up from North Fork Reservoir and extends for many miles into the national forest. The river's only downfall is its proximity to the state's largest metropolitan area, Portland, not to mention the fact that no special regulations exist here: I'm quite sure one could collect a thousand yards of discarded monofilament along a mile or so of riverbank. It always strikes me as odd that the people who fish the river the most seem to care for it the least.

The lower river offers lots of opportunity as well, but is primarily a boat show owing to extensive private property along the river. Below Estacada, the river is frequently over-run with hardware anglers, who have a short drive from the Portland area and who enjoy good fishing for runs of summer and winter steelhead along with the ever-popular spring chinook salmon. If you decide to try the lower river, do so between late May and mid-July and go mid-week. Three put-ins are located just below Estacada, including two at sprawling McIver State Park and the third being the county launch (Feldheimer) downstream about two miles.

To reach the put-ins, follow Clackamas River Hwy. (224) to Carver (about one mile south from the 224/212 interchange east of Clackamas). At Carver, take a right turn across the bridge and veer left on the south bank, following Springwater Road about nine miles to the park. Along the way you will pass the poorly marked turn-off to the Feldheimer Road launch. Bank anglers willing to do a little walking will find some good fly then you'll have to work hard at finding a spot where you can fish a run top to bottom. The fish are primarily small hatchery runs, weighing five to nine pounds, and they return to an ODFW hatchery on Eagle Creek. The folks at the hatchery can give you a pretty good idea of what kind of fishing to expect because they keep an accurate count of fish arriving at their trap.

Highway 224/211 crosses Eagle Creek almost three miles above its mouth about halfway between Estacada and Sandy. Bonnie Lure Park at the creek's mouth provides public access—turn west off the highway at the little village of Eagle Creek, north of the creek bridge. Otherwise, county roads follow the creek up to the hatchery. Another county park (Eagle Fern) is located above the first falls, about seven miles above the mouth. The hatchery is located another six or seven miles upstream—follow George Road on the north bank and watch for the signs.

Roaring River

A roadless tributary to the Clackamas, the Roaring River plunges through a scenic forest canyon accessible only by foot. The lower river holds a few summer steelhead; sometimes quite a few during years of strong runs. Otherwise the river is inhabited by small wild cutthroats. A Mt. Hood National Forest map will help you figure out the access points.

Molalla River

The Molalla River flows northwesterly out of the Cascade foothills south of Portland and northeast of Salem. This small river used to offer a fair run of hatchery summer steelhead during years with good numbers of fish passing over Willamette Falls. These are the same Skamania strain steelhead that run up the Willamette's other major tributaries, including the North and South Santiams and the McKenzie. Stocking of hatchery steelhead was discontinued in 1998, however, as part of a plan to protect and restore native runs of anadromous fish.

Although the summer steelhead are no longer available, the upper Mollala offers some fair fishing for small, native trout. Fly-angling pressure is usually light Several bridges cross the river east and southeast of the town of Molalla, while Molalla River Road follows the stream south towards its headwaters, where the better trout habitat exists. Roads parallel much of the river, providing excellent access.

Salmon River

Originating on Mt. Hood, the Salmon River forges a scenic path over tumbling falls and quiet evergreen forests on a short journey to its confluence with the Sandy River at Brightwood (on Hwy. 26). The Salmon River has long been popular among fly anglers, primarily for its run of summer steelhead and for the fact that a significant stretch of the river is fly-only water. Unfortunately for those who enjoyed warm summer days on the Salmon's elegant reaches, the hatchery steelhead programs were discontinued in 1998. Only a few wild summer steelhead ascend the river.

Though the hatchery summer steelhead are gone, the Salmon still offers some fair fishing for small, wild trout. With the Portland-metro area is but minutes away, anglers who fish mid-week can find plenty of open water. Moreover, the Salmon River's artificials-only reach is a hike-in affair, where those willing to walk the farthest will generally find the most solitude.

The elegant Molalla River offers a typically strong early summer run of hatchery steelhead.

The four miles of artificials-only water begin at Forest Road 2618, which crosses the river about five miles south of Zigzag. Turn south at the Welches Junction on Hwy. 26. The Salmon River Trail (Size 742) follow the river up to and beyond Final Falls (where upstream fish movement ends).

The upper reaches of the Salmon River, above Final Falls, offer good fishing for wild cutthroat on a strictly catch-and-release basis. This beautiful section of river includes several scenic falls, including Frustration Falls, Vanishing Falls, Little Niagara, Split Falls and Stein Falls. Forest Trail 742, from the bridge on Forest Road 2618, follows this entire length of river (about 10 miles). Another trail (665) reaches the river after a two-mile descent from Kinzel Lake Campground. At the upstream end of the Salmon River Trail, Linney Creek Campground is situated at river's edge, but above the campground, the river once again flows through a roadless canyon reach. The best access to the river above Linney Creek is by walking up from the campground or from a trail with several forks leading down from Fir Tree Campground on the north side.

To reach Fir Tree and Kinzel Lake campgrounds, follow Hwy. 26 to Still Creek Campground at Summit Meadow, from which FR2613 leads five miles to Fir Tree Campground and another five miles to Kinzel Lake. The Salmon River Meadows area, part of which is more or less adjacent to Hwy. 26 at Wapinitia Pass is paralleled at a distance on the south by the Pacific Crest Trail and on the north by FR2656 (the Trillium Lake Road). Be sure to consult the Mt. Hood National Forest Map or the Zigzag Ranger District Map.

Zigzag River

The tumultuous little Zigzag River tumbles for more than 10 miles off the flanks of Mt. Hood, dumping into the Sandy River at the town of Zigzag on Hwy. 26. The river is home to a modest run of hatchery summer steelhead that arrive between late May and August. Fishing peaks from late June through early September. This is high-gradient pocket and plunge-pool water where a six- or seven-weight outfit rigged with a floating line will do the trick. A few beautiful pools and runs are included as well. As with all our steelhead rivers, spiked boots or cleats of some kind should be considered mandatory. The best sections of the river are accessible from Hwy. 26 and a few short spur roads.

Sandy River

The Sandy River drains Mt. Hood and the surrounding region and is one of the most significant rivers in northwestern Oregon in terms of its production of anadromous fish. Of primary interest to fly anglers are the river's runs of both summer and winter steelhead.

Heavily fished by gear anglers, the Sandy flows from the slopes of Mt. Hood, picks up several major tributaries and eventually joins the Columbia near Troutdale, just east of Portland. Its proximity to Oregon's largest metropolitan area makes the Sandy a crowded place much of the time, especially when winter steelhead and chinook salmon arrive.

Nonetheless, good fly water abounds and perhaps the river's most unheralded fishery is for summer steelhead in the upper river. Most fly-angling pressure is concentrated above Marmot Dam, located about halfway between the communities of Sandy and Brightwood. Plenty of good fly water awaits below Marmot Dam, but so do plenty of plunkers and drift fishermen. Above Brightwood and the mouth of the Salmon River, the Sandy offers lots of nice fly water and pressure diminishes when Highway 26 turns away from the river at Zigzag.

The summer steelhead arrive from May through August, with peak fishing in July and September in the upper river. Winter fish, most from eight to ten pounds, ascend the river between December and March. The winter run is usually quite robust and although a minority of the fish are taken above Marmot Dam, the upper river often runs reasonably clear if the freezing level drops to 3,000 feet or a little more.

The upper Sandy is easily accessed by roads leading off Hwy. 26 upstream from the town of Sandy. Below Sandy, the lower river is paralleled in places by city and county roads, but the better access is by drift boat. Popular drifts run from Dodge Park near Sandy down to Oxbow Park east of Gresham or Dabney Park in Troutdale.

Willamette Zone High Lakes

The west slope of the Cascade Mountain Range offers countless high lakes that have been stocked with trout. In some lakes, these trout reproduce naturally; in others, populations are maintained by regular stockings of rainbow or brook trout. A few lakes have native cutthroat trout. Many of these lakes lie within the confines of the Mt. Jefferson and Three Sisters wilderness areas. Many others are drive-in or hike-in lakes that lie outside wilderness boundaries.

The best way to determine what kind of fish are in these myriad lakes is to first study a wilderness or national forest map and then contact ODFW in the Salem or Eugene office with a few specific lakes in mind. Ask the ODFW personnel to look up stocking records for the lakes in question.

Lakes with natural reproduction of brook trout or cutthroat are frequently over-populated with stunted versions of these fish. Pamelia Lake, a beautiful water in the Mt. Jefferson Wilderness, is the classic example of this: For years the ODFW allowed a 30-trout bag limit in hopes of controlling the rapidly reproducing cutthroat.

Often the larger fish are found in remote lakes with no natural reproduction, especially if you visit such lakes three to five years after the last stocking took place.

NORTHWEST ZONE

Only in recent years have fly anglers become a common sight on the numerous steelhead and salmon rivers that drain the coastal mountains of northwestern Oregon. Historically, these productive waters teemed with chinook, coho and chum salmon along with winter steelhead and sea-run cutthroat. Many were heavily fished by local hardware anglers and to this day, when the fish "are in" so to speak, the hordes arrive to fish elbow to elbow at the many popular roadside pools on rivers such as the Trask, Wilson, Nestucca, Nehalem and Salmon.

Yet all along Oregon's northwest coast, fly anglers in pursuit of everything from little resident cutthroat to chinook salmon and winter steelhead can find quiet places on productive streams. Increasingly, Oregon's coastal waters are managed to protect and hopefully enhance wild fish populations. Catch-and-release regulations are in effect for wild winter steelhead all along the coast. Significantly, stocking of legal-size trout in coastal streams has been halted and catch-and-release regulations implemented on the wild trout. These new trout regulations are aimed at restoring depressed populations of sea-run and resident cutthroat trout.

Trout-fishing can in fact be very productive on the small streams draining the coastal mountains and with the meat-hunting crowds divested of their motivation by catch-and-release rules, trout anglers can find peace and quiet along stretches of certain creeks that were rather heavily fished during the put-and-take days of the past. The resident cutthroat tend to run small, with foot-long specimens considered trophies; the sea-run variety, called "bluebacks" by some, can reach 20 inches or more, although 12- to 16-inch fish are typical.

After spending the summer feeding in the ocean and estuaries, these sea-run cutthroat return to the rivers during the late summer and fall. The name "harvest trout" derives from the timing of their arrival. Typically, the first fall freshet brings a rush of bluebacks into and above tidewater on most streams and by late September they are well-distributed.

Once abundant coastwide and common in virtually every coastal stream from the largest river to the smallest of year-round creeks, the sea-run cutthroat population has fallen on hard times for reasons not clearly understood. Certainly the devastation of their spawning habitat has had a profound effect: Countless acres of coastal forest is owned by private timber companies, virtually all of it having long been clear-cut with little regard for the tiny rivulets that serve as natal streams for ocean-going fishes like the sea-run cutthroat.

The blueback's future is in question and only in recent years has its life history been pieced together by fisheries biologists, who still don't completely understand this unique creature. In-stream habitat improvement projects are underway on many coastal streams, but it remains to be seen if these efforts can mitigate watershed-wide habitat crises. What's more, scientists are only beginning to understand relationships between relative ocean conditions and anadromous fish populations. Meanwhile, the clock keeps ticking on the sea-run cutthroat that for many years comprised a favorite fishery for many Oregon fly anglers.

In recent times, north coast fly anglers focus much of their attention on winter steelhead. The Northwest Zone includes some productive fly streams, including the Salmonberry River, Kilchis River, Nehalem River and Drift Creek. A few coastal rivers offer runs of summer steelhead and chief among these is the Siletz, whose upper reaches are the domain of fly anglers.

The Tillamook-area streams attract fly anglers in search of chinook and chum salmon. The Kilchis and Miami rivers are the traditional favorites for chum salmon, while the Trask and Wilson offer strong runs of fall chinook. Even among fly anglers, snagging seems to be the preferred method of hooking chinook salmon on the coast, so I hesitate even to talk about the fishery. This is not to say that snaggers dominate the fly-angling scene on the salmon rivers of Tillamook Bay, but casual observers and seasoned veterans alike would be forced to admit that for a fair share of the fly-rodders, fishing ethics often take a back seat to getting a 40-pound fish on the end of the line by whatever means necessary. Snagging and fishing the redds in no way resembles fair chase.

In addition to the ever-popular anadromous fish rivers and streams, the north coast offers little-known opportunities for saltwater fly fishing. A few free-spirited fly anglers pursue redtail surfperch (pinkfins) on the sandy beaches up and down the coast; others fish the jetties for rockfish and other bottom-dwelling species.

What's more, the central and northern Oregon coast features some productive warm-water fisheries for largemouth bass and sunfish. In fact, the big lakes between Florence and Coos Bay—Siltcoos, Tahkenitch and Tenmile—have become destination fisheries for serious bass anglers. While these lakes are not covered in this guide, they are nonetheless worth a look if you enjoy fishing for largemouth bass. All told, the Northwest Zone packs a lot of year-round opportunity into a thin slice of western Oregon.

Dave Hughes and Ted Leeson fishing the Siletz River for sea-run cutthroat trout.   JIM SCHOLLMEYER PHOTO

Siuslaw River

Traditionally, the Siuslaw was one of the top central-coast streams for sea-run cutthroat, but the fishery is nowhere near what it once was. Still a fair sea-run fishery remains, as do fair to good fisheries for winter steelhead, chinook salmon and shad.

The Siuslaw originates near Cottage Grove south of Eugene and meanders for many miles before reaching Lake Creek, one of its major tributaries. The river below Lake Creek is of most interest to fly anglers looking for anadromous fish. Terminal-gear anglers fish the tidewater section by boat, primarily for chinook salmon during the fall; fly anglers can cover some of the same water for sea-run cutthroat.

The reach from Mapleton up to Lake Creek is best for both steelhead and shad. Steelhead arrive December through March; shad in May and early June. Much of the river is accessible by foot from pull-outs along the road above Mapleton (Route 36). This section is also floatable. Launches are located at Swiss Home at the mouth of Lake Creek, at Tide Wayside and Farnham Landing below Swiss Home, and at Mapleton. Additional ramps are located upstream, north and south of Hwy. 126, an area that puts out fair numbers of winter fish during good years.

The shad fishery on the Siuslaw can be very productive if your timing is good. Late May generally offers the best fishing, especially when a dry spell offers reasonably low-water conditions. The best shad water for fly anglers lies between Mapleton and Rainrock a few miles above.

Lake Creek

A productive stream for winter steelhead, Lake Creek flows through Triangle Lake northwest of Eugene and joins the Siuslaw at Swiss Home. The steelhead fishing peaks from late January through March, with some big three-salt fish available. Road access is not particularly good owing to extensive private property, but this large creek is boatable.

The uppermost put-in is the ODFW pole slide at Greenleaf Creek on Hwy. 36 about four miles below Triangle Lake. A mid-drift ramp (gravel) is located at Deadwood about eight miles down from the Greenleaf put-in and additional ramps are located at the mouth of the creek (Indiola Landing) and down the Siuslaw at Tide Wayside. Lake Creek includes a couple of hazardous areas, so scout the drift first or go with someone who knows the river.

To reach Lake Creek from the Willamette Valley, follow Hwy. 36 from just south of Junction City to Triangle Lake and the creek. You can also take Hwy. 126 west out of Eugene and turn north onto Stagecoach Road east of Mapleton or onto Hwy. 36 at Mapleton. From the coast, follow Hwy. 126 from Florence to Mapleton and then head north on Hwy. 36.

Big Creek, Rock Creek, Tenmile Creek, Bob's Creek

Located south of the central-coast town of Yachats, these small streams feed directly into the Pacific and historically have provided fair to good fishing for sea-run cutthroat, winter steelhead and salmon. They are easily accessible, for the most part, off gravel access roads. The steelhead arrive between December and March, with the latter half of that time frame usually providing the best water conditions for fly anglers. Sea-run cutthroat enter these small streams upon the first rains of summer, especially if the rain coincides with high tides. The sea-run cutthroat populations have fallen on hard times lately, but these creeks are still worth exploring, especially since they afford an opportunity to hook cutthroat practically from the beach.

Alsea River

Historically, the Alsea River offered one of Oregon's best runs of sea-run cutthroat and was heavily fished by a small but dedicated lot of fly anglers. The sea-runs—all along the Oregon Coast—have fallen on hard times, but the Alsea remains a good bet for these fish and also for winter steelhead.

Sea-run cutthroat from the Alsea River.

The Alsea gathers its headwaters in the Coast Range southwest of Corvallis. Its two forks, the South Fork and North Fork, converge at the little town of Alsea and from there the river winds its way gradually toward the coast, finally surrendering to the Pacific at Waldport. Major tributaries include Five Rivers, Drift Creek and Fall Creek. The entire river is accessible by good roads, at least on the stretches that are not surrounded by private property. Highway 34 follows the river from Waldport to the South Fork, while forest roads access both forks.

Expect the first sea-run cutthroat to arrive in the lower river by July, with the first fall freshet moving fish above tide-water (usually sometime between early August and early September). The best early fishing is by boat on the lower river, from above the town of Tidewater downstream. Much of this reach is bordered by private property, so a boat is a virtual necessity. As this is a low-gradient tide-water stretch, you will want a motor for anything more than very short excursions. Myriad boat launches are available, all of which are privately operated and most of which require a modest launch fee. The uppermost private launch is near Hellion Rapids some 15 miles east of Waldport and a few miles east of Tidewater.

Bank access improves as you move upriver from Tidewater and all of the nine ramps above Hellion Rapids are public facilities operated by the county, the Forest Service and the BLM. Bank anglers and those drifting above the river upstream of tidal influence will find sea-runs in the Alsea shortly after the first fall freshet. Look for a day or two of rain, give the fish one to three days to move upriver, and then have at them as far upstream as Alsea, with the best reaches from Five Rivers down. Pay special attention to the mouths of tributary streams, including Fall Creek and Five Rivers.

Winter steelhead arrive between December and April, with the run of hatchery fish peaking around the first of February and the wild run peaking from mid-March through mid-April. Bait and hardware anglers do well between late December and early March, but fly anglers are a rare sight on the mainstem Alsea, perhaps owing to a lack of classic fly water. Still, the latter part of the season is a good time for fly anglers who choose low-water conditions at mid-week. Fishing pressure slacks off some by late February and fly anglers can continue to take bright fish into March.

By late winter, steelhead have entered both the North and South forks in numbers sufficient to attract a few fly anglers. The North Fork, below the hatchery, offers the best fly water. This is small-water fishing and can be quite productive during good years. Most of the water downstream from the Hwy. 34 bridge flows through private property, although there are two county parks. Access to private land by permission of the landowners can be worth the effort. The North Fork is generally open up to the hatchery, but check current regulations on both forks.

Five Rivers

A major tributary to the Alsea, Five Rivers offers winter steelhead and sea-run cutthroat, with the timing and composition of the runs about the same as in the Alsea. Much of the stream is bordered by private property, but anglers can either ask permission or ferret out a few nice runs and pools accessible to the public. The steelhead fishery extends to the mouth of Green River. Sea-run cutthroat fishing peaks in September and October, primarily in the lower two miles of the river downstream from the Lobster Creek confluence. Five Rivers Road follows a length of the river. The turn-off (Five Rivers Bridge) is at the county boat launch on the Alsea, 20 miles east of Waldport on Hwy. 34.

Lobster Creek

A tributary to Five Rivers, Lobster Creek flows through extensive private property, limiting access to its small runs of sea-run cutthroat and winter steelhead. Timing of the runs is the same as for Five Rivers. Turn south on Five Rivers Bridge, 20 miles east of Waldport, then turn left on Lobster Valley Road. Good fishing for small native cutthroat is available on the upper reaches of Lobster Creek and its tributaries.

Drift Creek (Alsea Tributary)

Joining the Alsea River from the north, at the top end of Alsea Bay, Drift Creek meanders a lengthy southwesterly journey through the Coast Range and through an extensive and hard-to-reach designated roadless area. Native winter steelhead ascend the creek between January and March; sea-run cutthroat—in limited numbers these days—arrive with the fall freshets. Both chinook and coho salmon spawn in Drift Creek as well. The coho are protected in this watershed.

The lower end of the river is of interest primarily to blueback anglers, or at least it was when the runs were strong. This is primarily a boat show as the lower river flows through private property. The Drift

Creek Roadless Area above, however, is lightly fished due to its remoteness and the fact that you must descend steep trails to reach the creek. Drift Creek Road turns east off Hwy. 101 just north of the bridge over Alsea Bay at Waldport. Consult the Siuslaw National Forest Map for directions to the spur roads, but check with the Forest Service before tackling any of the spur roads during the winter season.

The wilderness stretch offers good summer fishing for wild cutthroat, as does the upper river. However, Drift Creek's upper reaches are primarily owned by Georgia Pacific. These private timber lands are generally open on weekends only.

Beaver Creek

A medium-sized stream entering the Pacific at Ona Beach, eight miles south of Newport, Beaver Creek once offered good fishing for sea-run cutthroat. The sea-run population is reduced now, but anglers can still find a few fish in Beaver Creek, which also offers a small run of winter steelhead. The lower few miles of the creek, within tidewater, are most popular and are accessible only by boat. A good launch is located just east of the Hwy. 101 bridge. Turn east on Beaver Creek Road just north of the creek.

Siletz River

One of Oregon's top coastal streams for summer steelhead, the Siletz—its North Fork at least—features a fly-only section where anglers can fish classic dry-line tactics on as pretty a stream as one could diagram. In addition, the Siletz ranks among the most heavily fished rivers on the coast for its winter steelhead and chinook runs. Traditionally, this lengthy river system has also been a productive sea-run cutthroat river.

The Siletz gathers its headwaters from the Coast Range west of Monmouth and Falls City and much of the upper river and the North and South forks flow through private timber lands. The river makes a

Siletz River.

JIM SCHOLLMEYER PHOTO

meandering southwesterly swing before veering north and west again before reaching the Pacific at Siletz Bay just south of Lincoln City.

Of primary interest to most fly anglers is the fly-only water on the North Fork Siletz, which is open from its confluence with the South Fork up to the old Stott Mountain Bridge. This is a beautiful gin-clear, small-water river complete with easily readable runs, pools and tailouts. Many of the gliding runs and glassy tailouts are perfectly suited to skating dry flies. Otherwise, try classic wet flies, fished on a floating line.

The upper reaches of the main Siletz, below the confluence of the forks, offers lots of good fly water as well. Despite the river's popularity, week-day fly anglers can usually find plenty of elbow room during the summer-run season, even in the ever-popular gorge upstream from Moonshine Park. A majority of gear anglers are content to spend their entire morning fishing one of the easily accessible holes, leaving lots of shallow fly water to those willing to walk and wade. The road that accesses the gorge is on land owned by Georgia Pacific (Upper Farm Road) and is subject to closure on occasion. You can check by calling Georgia Pacific at 541/336-3819.

The summer steelhead begin entering the Siletz by mid-May. Peak fishing runs from mid-June through early July. Fishing picks up again with the first good freshets in August or September and can last until the seasonal rains begin. The Siletz summer run is comprised of about 90 percent hatchery fish.

The upper reaches of the Siletz, including the North and South forks, have long been good places to get your car broken into. Anglers would be well-advised not to leave valuables in the vehicle.

The winter run begins in December and lasts through March. The gorge, above Moonshine Park, is popular with both fly and gear anglers. Fish stack up in this reach and bank access is good. Below Moonshine, the river is better for boaters, as bank access is limited. One of the best fly-angling runs is from Moonshine down to Twin Bridges (Sam's Creek Launch) below the town of Logsden, but this is also a popular drift for gear fishermen as well, so don't expect to have the river to yourself. You will find lots of good fly water on this scenic drift, but with the trip covering something like seven miles, a winter day can pass quickly. Only experienced oarsmen should attempt this drift, especially when the water drops to optimum levels for fly angling, exposing lots of boat-scraping rocks. This upper end of the river clears fast after a rain.

Several additional launches are located along the rest of the river with popular drifts running from Twin Bridges down to Illahee Park in the town of Siletz, from Illahee around the big bend west of Siletz and down to Old Mill Park (the so-called Town Drift), from Old Mill Park down to the unimproved launch at Ojalla Bridge (bring a long rope), from Old Mill Park or Ojalla Bridge down to Morgan Park. This lower drift is a fair run for sea-run cutthroat because its lower end takes you down to tide-water. The upper drifts are better for steelheading.

The sea-run cutthroat fishery peaks in tidewater during July. The lower river is best fished by a boat with a motor. Look for structure in the form of snags, overhanging brush and current seams. When the freshets occur during August and September, the fish move upstream, often following spawning salmon. Downriver launches are located at several places: fee ramps at Sportsman's Landing and Coyote Rock RV Park a few miles up the Siletz River Road from Hwy. 101 and at Sunset Landing further upriver; a county launch (Strom's Landing) is located about 10 miles north of the town of Siletz, four miles downstream from Morgan park.

Drift Creek (Siletz Bay Tributary)

Large native winter steelhead are the main attraction on Drift Creek, which enters Siletz Bay about a mile north of the Siletz River Bridge on Hwy. 101 south of Lincoln City. Owing to catch-and-release regulations for wild steelhead, Drift Creek offers haven to both fish and fly fisher. Prior to the catch-and-release rules, gear and bait anglers took quite a few fish out of this small stream. During the early 1980s, for example, catches ran as high as 1,700 fish, with 500 or 600 being about average.

After the stocking of hatchery fish was discontinued and catch-and-release rules enacted, the kill rate and fishing pressure dropped. These

A beautiful native winter steelhead.

days (assuming wild-fish management continues), Drift Creek is a decidedly pleasant place to fish and a fairly productive stream for winter steelhead fly angling.

The lower half of Drift Creek is accessible by walking in from Drift Creek Road (Forest Primary Route 19) and by walking above or below the Drift Creek Camp. Drift Creek Road turns west off Hwy. 101 south of Lincoln City, about a mile north of the Siletz River Bridge at Kernville.

Winter steelhead enter the stream as early as December, but February and March are the best months. Sea-run cutthroat arrive after the first heavy rains in late summer or September, but their numbers appear to be highly reduced from decades past. A run of fall chinook salmon remains strong most years, peaking mid-autumn; anglers interested in pursuing the salmon can find mint-bright biters by fishing the lower river on a high tide.

Salmon River

The ever-popular Salmon River flows out of the Van Duzer Corridor along Highway 18 east of Lincoln City. Highway 101 crosses the Salmon about two miles above its mouth, which is overlooked on the north by massive Cascade Head. For the most part, the Salmon is no place for fly anglers when the fall chinook are in, at least that's my opinion. Its modest run of hatchery winter steelhead and its sea-run cutthroat run, however, are worth pursuing.

Most of the salmon anglers gather near the ODFW hatchery above Otis, often forming honest-to-God hordes; I've watched a fist-fight or two break out among the rowdies. Should you wish to shoulder in on the

Coastal estuary.

action, go mid-week or choose a second option: Fish the estuary on the west side of Hwy. 101.

Above the hatchery, however, fly anglers can find winter steelhead between December and February, sometimes as late as March. The gear anglers tend to concentrate at and below the hatchery, so if you take the time to ferret out a few good runs a little further upstream, you can find water all to yourself. Above Rose Lodge, the Salmon River is fairly accessible along the highway. Included on the Salmon are some nice gravel-bottom pools well-suited to swinging wet flies on sinking or sink-tip lines.

Sea-run cutthroat numbers are not what they used to be, but the fish still arrive after the first freshet in late summer or early fall. The lower river is best, from the little town of Otis down to the estuary. Adventurous fly anglers can hunt up an occasional salmon and a few sea-run in the estuary itself, below the 101 bridge. You can launch a boat from the Knight Park Ramp off Three Rocks Road, which turns west off Hwy. 101 about a mile north of the river. From the launch, motor back upstream and fish the river and the tidal creeks feeding it from the south. Move quietly and keep your eyes peeled for visible salmon, which often cruise the tidal creeks and the river itself. Obviously the run upriver should be made on the incoming tide.

Nestucca River

The Nestucca River, a coastal stream south of Tillamook, is one of Oregon's most popular steelhead streams, which may explain why many fly anglers give it a wide berth: it's hard to find a place to cast a fly when drift fishermen line the banks at every run and pool. However, if you look for out-of-the-way and less obvious runs and slots and fish during mid-week, the Nestucca can produce about as well as any of the coast rivers.

Its winter steelhead run is the Nestucca's most popular and heavily fished option. The summer steelhead run, while still heavily fished, leaves more room for fly anglers to operate much of the time, especially in the upper river, between Beaver and Elk Creek. During good years, the summer fish are rather abundant, but unfortunately, the doldrums of midsummer tend to afflict the Nestucca's steelhead with a serious case of

lockjaw. The first rainfall in late July or August tends to prompt a good bite for those who get to the river immediately. The same August freshets will bring sea-run cutthroat into tidewater and tempt the first fall chinook salmon to leave the bay and enter the lower river.

A sustained rain between late August and mid-September gets the salmon on the move and bright fish are sometimes willing to bite flies in the lower end of the river. Nestucca Bay itself can offer a chance at mint-bright chinook that will sometimes chase and eat small baitfish patterns and bonefish-style shrimp patterns. You will need a boat to look for salmon cruising the river channel, side channels and tidal creeks following a high tide. Early morning and evening are best. Launches are located at Pacific City and off Hwy. 101 at the Little Nestucca Bridge.

Both the summer and winter runs of steelhead are comprised mostly of hatchery fish. Summer fish commonly run five to seven pounds; winter fish reach six to ten pounds with a fair number of 10- to 15-pound fish available. Summer fish arrive between May and early July; winter fish from late December through March. For both runs, the water below 5th Bridge holds the most fish, but by July and late January, respectively, enough fish have wandered above 5th Bridge to make the effort worthwhile on the upper river, where bank access is best.

Between the little towns of Beaver on the north and Cloverdale on the south, bank access is available in places along Hwy. 101 and a few secondary roads. A drift boat is the better choice. Half a dozen launches are located along the river above Pacific City. This is the most popular reach on the river, so don't be surprised if your attempt to fish even a small run or pool from top to bottom is intruded upon time and again by plunkers.

Little Nestucca River

Primarily known for its winter steelhead, the Little Nestucca is a scenic little river that crosses Hwy. 101 just south of the southernmost turn-off to Pacific City. The Little Nestucca joins the Big Nestucca below town on a narrow estuary frequented in the winter by a protected flock of rare Aleutian Canada geese.

Fishing the lower Nehalem for sea-run cutthroat trout.   FRANK AMATO PHOTO

Steelhead enter the Little Nestucca between December and February with a few late arrivals coming in March. Late December through early February is the peak fishing period. The river is fairly heavily fished, more because of its excellent bank access than because of bountiful steelhead runs. In fact, with the hatchery allotment being phased out, the steelhead numbers are down substantially from years past.

The river is followed closely by a good paved road with plenty of curves. From the east, follow Highway 22 north from Grand Ronde/Valley Junction or south from Hebo. Near the tiny hamlet of Dolph, turn west on Little Nestucca Highway. From the west, follow Highway 101 to its junction with Little Nestucca Highway a mile or so south of the Brooton Road turn-off to Pacific City.

Three Rivers

A tributary of the Nestucca, Three Rivers is primarily of interest to gear fishermen, who fish its lower reaches for winter steelhead. Although paralleled by a good road, the river is largely locked up in private land for the first several miles above the mouth. Most of the pressure is concentrated at the Heart Attack Hole (Hatchery Hole), the S-curves and at the mouth.

Generally speaking, fly anglers have little chance to fish among the drift fishermen, who arrive in numbers sufficient that anglers must simply pick a spot and stay put. Sometimes, during weekdays when pressure is light (not very often), you may get a chance to fish through some productive water at the mouth. Don't count on it. In any case, the winter steelhead, mostly hatchery fish, arrive between late November and March. A few summer fish ascend the river as far up as the hatchery, but Three Rivers is closed from the hatchery weir to the mouth between June 1 and October 31. Because no summer fish are passed above the hatchery, no real opportunity exists for summer steelheading.

Tillamook River

The Tillamook River flows almost entirely through private property, leaving little access for anglers. Wild winter steelhead enter the river between December and March, but the run hardly compares to those in the Trask, Wilson and Kilchis. Potentially, the fishery of interest to fly anglers is the sea-run cutthroat run, which peaks during July and August. You will need a boat with a motor, which you can launch at Burton Frazier Ramp where Tillamook River Road crosses the river south of Tillamook. This is all tidewater, with minimal structure: Fish incoming tides and concentrate on log/stump structure, cut banks, and any other visible structure or cover.

Trask River

Like the Wilson River immediately to the north, the Trask River offers runs of both winter and summer steelhead, along with sea-run cutthroat and chinook salmon. The timing of the steelhead runs is similar to those on the Wilson, with the winter fish, most of which are wild, arriving from December through March and peaking January and February. Among the February-March fish are some trophy-size natives of 15 to 20 or more pounds. The modest summer steelhead run, comprised of hatchery fish, arrives from May through August and peaks during July.

Interestingly, while hatchery winter steelhead are common on the Trask, none are planted in the river, which is managed for its wild fish. The hatchery steelhead are likely strays from the nearby Wilson and perhaps other streams.

Fall chinook provide an important fishery on the Trask and this river is one of the region's most popular with fly anglers pursuing the salmon. The run peaks in November and when the fish are in and the river is at optimal levels, you'll have no trouble finding the productive areas: Just look for cars and anglers, with fly anglers often quite numerous.

Most of the time, at least during the steelhead runs, the Trask is less crowded than the Wilson and other area rivers. Access is not as easy on the Trask and the steelhead not so numerous. However, the chance to hook a huge native winter fish during February or March makes the Trask one of the top prospects on the north coast.

Among fly anglers, the mile-long stretch of river from the Dam Hole (popular with gear fishermen) up to Upper Peninsula has become quite popular. Locals often refer to this segment as the "Park Area." Included are two boat launches, but these should be considered take-outs for drifts from the upper river: Below the peninsula is one of the most hazardous stretches of river to be found on any of the Tillamook-area rivers: Don't even try floating through as you will likely lose the boat.

Lots of good fly water awaits those who drift the Trask. Among the most popular segments, and one ripe with fly water, is the two-mile drift from Cedar Creek to Loren's Drift (also called The Pig Farm and Hakenkrat's). The rough launch at Cedar Creek is located on Trask River Road about three miles up from Johnson Bridge: From Hwy. 6 (Wilson River Road) turn south on Olsen Road (about two miles east of Tillamook), follow Olsen down to Trask River Road and turn left. Cedar Creek is about three miles upriver. Loren's Drift is located on Chance Road, 5.5 miles from Tillamook. Take Long Prairie Road east off Hwy. 101 south of town or take Hwy. 6 to Olsen Road and cross the river at Johnson Bridge.

The next take-out below Loren's Drift is Lower Trask, located off Long Prairie Road just east of the 101 Bridge. For a long day's fishing, the lengthy drift from Cedar Creek to Lower Trask forces you to pass up lots of water, which is fine when the river is fairly busy. To allow more time for fishing on the lower reaches, put-in at Loren's Drift and float to Lower Trask.

The upper river, while seldom drifted, offers lots of fine fly water. Stone Camp Launch, a rarely used pole slide, offers access to the highest drift segment, with the take-outs being at Upper and Lower Peninsula, both ODFW gravel take-outs. The drift from Stone Camp covers two to 2.5 miles. Be sure to bring a strong, 100-foot rope for the Stone Camp Slide, which is an unusually steep affair. Last time I checked, Stone Camp Slide was unmarked: Turn right off Trask River Road onto a gravel spur just past Milepost 10.

For fly anglers, the Trask naturally fishes best at low water. Call the National Weather Service (503/261-9246) for river readings and listen for the Wilson River reading, by which you will have to estimate the Trask's height. Ideally, the water should be below or near four feet. You can generally count on the Trask to drop into shape about two days after a rainstorm, perhaps three or four days after a heavy storm.

Top to bottom, the Trask offers water of varying nature. Upriver you will find a predominance of bedrock reefs forming precipitous edges on deep pools. The tailouts form from the same reefs, but offer gravel-filled slots and channels where steelhead hold. Boulder-studded runs and riffles abound and become increasingly common as you move downriver. Once the Trask enters the Tillamook Valley and swings away from the road, the pastoral dairylands hide many gravel/cobblestone runs and pools that are easily fished with a fly rod.

The Trask's big natives, along with the hatchery fish, are susceptible to classic fly-rod techniques assuming you choose good fly water. Runs and tailouts from three to six feet deep are ideal. In the deeper water, swing a big wet fly on a high-density sink-tip or sinking head. For the gear-grabbing, boulder-strewn runs, some of which are avoided by hardware anglers who fear losing too much tackle, switch to a floating line or 10-foot sink-tip and use a leader of eight to 10 feet. On the business end, try a Comet pattern. In years past, I tied lots of flies for a tackle shop on the coast and invariably the local fly anglers purchased three winter steelhead patterns above all others: Boss Comet, Hot Orange Comet and Hot Pink Comet, respectively.

The upper reaches of the Trask, including the North Fork and the South Fork (and the East Fork) offer fair to good fishing for native, resident cutthroat in lightly pressured waters. However, the trout season is open only for about three weeks during May and June. The season framework protects juvenile salmon and steelhead. Be sure to consult current synopsis. Forest roads access these waters. Both forks have winter steelhead by mid- to late February and both have some small, but nice fly water accessible by road and bushwhacking. The upstream extent of the North Fork run is Bark Shanty Creek; the South Fork, Edwards Creek. All other tributaries are closed.

Winter steelhead fly fishing from a drift boat. (Don't wear red!)

Wilson River

One of the top steelhead and salmon streams on the north coast, the Wilson River is also among the most accessible and is therefore a popular destination. Nonetheless, good fly water abounds on the Wilson, especially upstream from Mills Bridge, where Hwy. 6 (Wilson River Road) crosses the river.

The Wilson's run of winter steelhead generally peaks in January, but the few low-water days of December can be productive as well. Look for water levels below five feet. Winter steelheading holds up through February, sometimes later. Should the water drop below 4.5 feet, fly anglers can find lots of runs and pools devoid of drift fishermen.

Access from the highway is good, though precipitous in places. A drift boat offers the advantage of fishing from both banks and avoiding the popular highway holes where hardware anglers congregate. The Siskeyville to Mills Bridge drift covers less than three miles; for a longer drift, put-in upriver at the Herd Hole, which, like Siskeyville, is a pole-slide launch. The river offers straight-forward boating, but be careful: At low water levels optimal for fly angling, lots of rocks are exposed, especially in the Rock Garden about halfway between Siskeyville and Mills Bridge. Two additional take-outs are located downriver from Mills Bridge: The Donaldson Road access, a private fee-launch, is about 2.5 miles below Mills Bridge and the Sollie Smith ODFW ramp lies another 2.5 miles below Donaldson, off Wilson River Loop Road.

If you're fishing without the benefit of a drift boat, you will find good road access within Tillamook State Forest, upstream from Milepost 12. You'll have to scramble down the banks in places, but you will find lots of gravel pull-outs along the highway.

In addition to its good runs of winter steelhead, the Wilson offers summer steelhead from May through September, along with sea-run cutthroat from late July through mid-autumn. The summer steelhead fishery peaks in July, with the stretch of river from Sollie Smith up to Mills Bridge being most popular; however, the summer run extends all the way up to Jones Creek and fly anglers can fish some beautiful pools between Mills Bridge and the county park upriver at Fall Creek. The summer fish are all hatchery steelhead, while some 30 percent of the winter run are wild fish, which must be released.

A typically robust run of fall chinook arrives from October through November. Fly anglers who time the run right and know the river, can find fresh chinook arriving on high tides. Once in a while they grab flies presented at their level; other times, a few from the fly angling community join the ranks of the snaggers. As for the sea-run cutthroat, whose numbers are depressed from decades past, try the lower river, below Mills Bridge, between mid-July and mid-September.

Access to the Wilson River above Mills Bridge is mostly from Hwy. 6, which departs Hwy. 26 (Sunset Highway) west of Portland and follows the river most of the way to Tillamook. The Sollie Smith Access is located on Wilson River Loop Road, which turns north off the highway about two miles east of Tillamook. The fee access at Donaldson is located at the end of Donaldson Road, which exits the highway about 1.5 miles east of Wilson River Loop Road.

Kilchis River

For quite a number of years, the lovely little Kilchis River north of Tillamook ranked as Oregon's top chum salmon river for fly anglers. The chum salmon runs remain, but in a substantially reduced fashion—a situation that a few years ago prompted ODFW to curtail the catch-and-kill season and open the chum runs only to limited catch-and-release fishing.

The catch-and-release regulations are a blessing for fly anglers even if the depressed runs are not. For now the river is devoid of the meat-hunting hordes; the catch-and-release folks, whether they be fly anglers or hardware anglers, seem to be a more congenial lot. The chum season generally extends from mid-September through mid-November. Should early fall rains bring fish into the river around the beginning of the chum season, fly anglers can fish over bright salmon. Later, you have to sort through the pools to find the fresh arrivals: Hooking chum salmon that have been in the river for a while bears little resemblance to sport.

The Kilchis offers runs of chinook, both spring and fall, along with sea-run cutthroat in limited numbers, but perhaps the fishery of most interest to serious fly anglers is the run of winter steelhead between December and March. The Kilchis is a small river, so fly anglers would be well-served to avoid crowded weekends and to wait for water so low that the hardware crowd goes elsewhere. Bank access is limited on the Kilchis and those places that are accessible are typically clogged up with bait anglers. A drift boat is a good idea.

The Kilchis offers two drifts: From Kilchis Park down to the Logging Bridge or to Hwy. 101 take-out and from the Logging Bridge to 101. Both drifts cover about three miles. Kilchis Park (Kilchis River Recreation Area) is located at the end of Kilchis River Road, which turns off Hwy. 101 a few miles north of Tillamook. The logging bridge is about halfway up the road, just upstream from the gravel quarry.

The scenic Kilchis River offers one of Oregon's few remaining runs of chum salmon along with good runs of winter steelhead and chinook salmon.

Chum salmon on the Miami River.

Miami River

Northernmost of Tillamook Bay's large tributary streams, the Miami River empties into Miami Cove near Garibaldi. For fly anglers, the Miami's run of chum salmon is the big attraction, although the size of the run is substantially reduced from just a few years ago. Winter steelhead comprise the other fishery of interest to fly anglers, with the run extending from January through March. The river runs mostly through private land, but a few stretches offer access from the highway easement and in years past, certain landowners along the river have offered access for a modest fee. Check with the ODFW in Tillamook for the latest word on access.

Salmonberry River

The beautiful Salmonberry River provides an opportunity for adventurous fly anglers to pursue wild winter steelhead in a fairly remote coastal range stream. Steelhead enter the river as early as December, but the bulk of the run arrives from mid-February through March. The best fishing usually occurs during the latter half of March (the season closes March 31). As with any coastal river, water levels change quickly and during wet winters, good fly-fishing opportunities can be restricted to a handful of low-water days. During other years, a week-long spell of reasonably dry weather might occur at any time during the season.

The Salmonberry flows about 18 miles before joining the Nehalem River 12 miles south of Elsie. Lower Nehalem Road crosses the Salmonberry's mouth. Here anglers can hike up the river along the railroad tracks (watch for trains). The most productive waters are found in the lower half of the river below the confluence of the North Fork. Lower Nehalem Road turns south off Highway 26 at Elsie, about two miles west of Jewell Junction. If you are arriving from the coast, turn east on Route 53 between Nehalem and Wheeler, drive about two miles until you pass Nehalem Bay Winery (a mandatory stop) and just past the river turn right (south) on Miami River Road. After a mile, turn left on Foss Road and follow the Nehalem up to the Salmonberry. The upper river, above the forks, can be reached via Camp 10 Road off Hwy. 26. Consult a Tillamook County map for specifics. By accessing the upper river, anglers can fish downstream from Pennoyer Creek.

The Salmonberry is small water, combining pocket-water with elegant runs, glides and pools. Classic patterns, including Spey-styles, Practitioners and Marabou flies, will take fish in the pools, tailouts and deeper runs for those proficient in using sink-tip and sinking lines. Fished on a floating line with a long leader, Comets and other weighted patterns can be swung through the rocky glides.

A modest but fishable run of sea-run cutthroat enters the river by late July. The best fishing is in the lower two miles, especially after a freshet in August or early September. Try a Borden Special, Purple Joe or other classic blueback pattern.

North Fork Nehalem River

Don't confuse the North Fork Nehalem with the Nehalem River, as the North Fork is generally the better stream for fly anglers seeking hatchery and wild winter steelhead. The North Fork's run begins in early December and peaks between late December and late January. The best fishing extends from the head of the tidewater a few miles north of the town of Nehalem upstream to God's Valley Creek (a few miles east of Route 53). The river is closed above Hamlet Road and the region-wide catch-and-release regulations apply to all wild steelhead.

Some of the best fly water for walk-in anglers is located above the Nehalem River Fish Hatchery. Only wild fish are allowed to pass through the ladder at Waterhouse Falls, so anglers fishing above the falls (located just below Route 53) and east of the highway, must release their catch. Lots of private property abuts the river, but east of Route 53 a gravel road provides good access. Public access is available at the hatchery, but fly anglers won't find much room to work on a typical day.

You can access the west bank, below the hatchery, on property owned by Longview Fiber. Turn west on Soapstone Mountain Road just north of the Route 53 bridge. The first left off this road accesses the river below the hatchery. Or continue straight ahead to reach the rapids.

Drifters can put-in at the hatchery, but be forewarned: The upper half of the float includes some difficult rapids, which can be all but impassable when the water drops to the low levels most conducive to fly angling. For floating the upper river, some anglers use rubber rafts rather than risk banging up a drift boat. Two additional ramps are located down river. The first is a fee launch on Jim Erickson's property (located at about Milepost 11 on the Clatsop/Tillamook County Line); the second is the Aldervale Public Ramp about two miles further downstream. The short drift from Erickson's to Aldervale is easy, but the better fly water is found above. As of this writing, Erickson's launch fee is $7 and a shuttle service is available.

The limited access and the difficult drift on the North Fork combine to create ideal conditions for fly anglers looking for uncrowded waters with good numbers of winter steelhead. That is not to say the river is never crowded because it does draw lots of attention on weekends. However, if you fish mid-week and fish the smaller pools and runs between the popular drift-fishing holes, you can cover lots of productive water without much company. Check with ODFW in Tillamook and at the hatchery for further access recommendations.

The North Fork usually offers a good run of sea-run cutthroat during August and September with the best fishing being in tidewater in the lower river.

Nehalem River

This expansive north coast river steers a 115-mile course through the coast range, following an exaggerated horseshoe-shaped path and crossing Hwy. 26 twice before surrendering to the Pacific at Nehalem Bay. With its runs of salmon, steelhead and cutthroat, the Nehalem draws lots of attention from anglers.

However, compared to the Salmonberry, one of its tributaries, and the North Fork Nehalem, the Nehalem itself rates only fair to poor as a steelhead fishery for fly anglers. In fact, the most popular stretch of fly water on the Nehalem is the mouth of the Salmonberry, even though a few steelhead make it as far upstream as river mile 110 above Timber.

The Nehalem's run of winter steelhead, all of them wild after hatchery releases were discontinued in 1994, enter the river as early as the first of December and continue through the winter. Some of these fish are behemoths up to 20 pounds. Peak fishing is during March or during low-water periods in February. Watch for river gauge readings below six feet, preferably closer to four feet for optimal fly-angling conditions.

The lower end of the Nehalem, from the Salmonberry River downstream, is most popular with steelheaders. Bank access is limited, but drifters can float the lower end of this stretch, launching at Beaver Slide near Lost Creek and exiting the river at Roy Creek Park six miles downstream on Foss Road. A private fee ramp is located a short distance further downstream at Mohler Sand & Gravel.

The Nehalem offers a good sea-run cutthroat fishery beginning about mid-July and continuing through September. The best fishing is from the mouth of the Salmonberry downstream to the mouth of the North Fork below tidewater. Additionally, wild resident cutthroat are available throughout much of the river. Try the Vernonia to Elsie stretch or the Elsie to Cook Creek reach. The latter section is accessible from Lower Nehalem River Road and from Cook Creek Road. Study a good map to figure out access between Elsie and Vernonia. Small boats can launch or exit at the highway bridges and ODFW has several public ramps, one near Pittsburg and another ramp, the Pope-Meeker Drift Boat Access, is located near Elsie, north of Hwy. 26, off Fishhawk Falls Road. Luukinen Road Access, well-signed on Hwy. 26, lies south of the highway just east of Elsie.

Cook Creek

Cook Creek is an important tributary to the lower Nehalem, entering the river about 2.5 miles below Nehalem Falls. Wild steelhead ascend Cook Creek between early December and mid-January. A five-mile reach from the Nehalem up to the South Fork of Cook Creek is open until the end of March. Cook Creek Road parallels the stream.

Rock Creek

A lengthy tributary of the upper Nehalem, Rock Creek begins just south of Hwy. 26, east of Jewell Junction, and enters the river at Vernonia. A few wild winter steelhead are available during February and March, but the trout fishery is probably of more interest. Wild resident cutthroat (and probably sea-runs as well) inhabit the stream in good numbers.

A big cutthroat would stretch to 13 inches, but owing to extensive private property, angling pressure is light and a fly angler willing to knock on doors can have a day of small-stream fishing all to him- or herself. Anglers can also walk in from Sunset Wayside on Hwy. 26 or walk upstream from Keasey. Get a good county map before setting off on a journey to Rock Creek.

Humbug Creek

Humbug Creek flows more-or-less parallel to Hwy. 26 before emptying into the Nehalem at Elsie. This is a fair to good stream for wild cutthroat to 14 inches. The East Fork, north of Hwy. 26, is followed by East Humbug Road. The West Fork is walk-in-only and therefore receives little pressure. The one mile of Humbug Creek between the West and East forks follows closely beside Hwy. 26. Downstream of the East Fork, private property limits access.

Necanicum River

Underrated as a fly-rod steelhead stream, the lovely little Necanicum River follows the west end of Hwy. 26 and then flows north along Hwy. 101 into Seaside, where the river meets the Pacific. Winter steelhead, both wild and hatchery, ascend the Necanicum from December through early March.

Good fly water abounds in the nine-mile section from the South Fork along Hwy. 26 to Beerman Creek Ramp just south of Seaside. Despite its proximity to two major highways, the Necanicum offers little bank access because of extensive private property along its banks. Your best bet is to drift from Klootchie Creek Park (on Hwy. 26) down to Beerman. Or you

A typically small coastal stream.

Mouth of the Necanicum at Seaside.

can make a short, easy drift of about three miles from Klootchie down to a fee ramp adjacent to Johnson Construction just south of the Hwy. 101 bridge. Bank anglers can fish a short reach of river between the South Fork and Klootchie Creek Park, where the largest Sitka spruce in the U.S. resides (a giant of a tree, well worth the stop).

During low-flow winters, adventurous fly anglers can take a crack at steelhead that congregate in tidewater in the town of Seaside. The 12th Avenue Bridge is a popular spot at such times, but anglers can find other bank access above and below 12th Avenue. During high-flow winters, the fish don't congregate so the tidewater fishery never really develops.

Sea-run cutthroat enter the Necanicum during summer and fall. During July and August, try the section from Beerman Creek through the Seaside Golf Course. Drop a small boat in at Beerman (located along Hwy. 101 south of Seaside) and then row or motor back after fishing down to the golf course (or make arrangements to take out at one of the private moorings in town). This is perfect canoe water. The Beerman Access is nothing more than a gravel pull-off just south of Seaside—look for ODFW signs posted on the tree, below which is a dirt trail, five or six feet wide, leading a few yards to the river. This is small water during the summer and you may need to walk the boat through a couple of gentle, shallow riffles below the put-in. After the first fall freshet in September, fish the Klootchie Creek to Beerman reach.

Klaskanine River

During years with strong runs, the Klaskanine is a fair stream for winter steelhead, but this small river tends to be heavily fished by gear anglers. Perhaps of more interest to fly anglers—again during years when runs are strong—is the river's sea-run cutthroat fishery, which begins even before the first freshet in late summer.

By mid-July, sea-run cutthroat are available in tidewater, which is accessible from Klaskanine Park off Saddle Mountain Road: Follow Hwy. 202 south out of Astoria from the east end of Young's Bay Bridge. You can also put-in at Tide Point Ramp (two miles south from Hwy. 101 on Hwy. 202) and motor up to the mouth of the river, but make sure you study the tides first. After the first freshet (typically sometime during August), the cutthroat will move upstream, where anglers can find them as far upstream as the ODFW hatchery.

Winter steelhead enter the river by early December, with peak fishing between late December and mid-January. The run is primarily of hatchery origin, although the South Fork Klaskanine, which is virtually unfishable due to extensive private timberlands, hosts a run comprised of perhaps 30 percent wild fish. In any case, the steelhead fishery extends from tidewater up to the hatchery on the North Fork. This entire reach is

fairly accessible from Hwy. 202 (Nehalem Highway), but be sure to ask before crossing private lands.

Hatcheries on the North and South forks produce coho salmon, which provide a fishery during the fall, and fall chinook arrive about the same time. Hatchery jacks are quite common most years. Wild resident cutthroat trout are available above the hatchery on the North Fork and in the South Fork. They average eight to 12 inches and are lightly fished, partly due to limited access.

Young's River

The Young's River is a small cutthroat stream near Astoria. Above its falls, the river is restricted to artificial flies and lures. Small wild cutthroat abound and are lightly fished owing to poor access. As of this writing the private forest roads along the river are open only during deer season.

Clatskanie River

A small river entering the Columbia west of Rainier, the Clatskanie offers fair to good fishing for wild cutthroat trout in its upper reaches and tributaries and spotty fishing for sea-run cutthroat in its lower half. The lower part of the river flows mostly through private land, but the tidewater reach can be fished by boat. An improved ramp is located in Clatskanie. Above tidewater, a knock on a door should get you permission to fish.

The best section for the resident cutthroats, which span eight to 12 inches, is from Miller Creek up to Schaffer Road. Most of this reach is easy access. The easiest route to the upper river is from Apiary Road, which heads south from Hwy. 30 a few miles west of Rainier, and eventually intersects Schaffer Road, which in turn parallels the stream.

The Clatskanie gets a modest to good run of winter steelhead as well, with the fishery peaking between mid-January and late March. When the fish are in, expect a crowd.

The Necanicum River often offers fair to good prospects for winter steelhead and sea-run cutthroat.

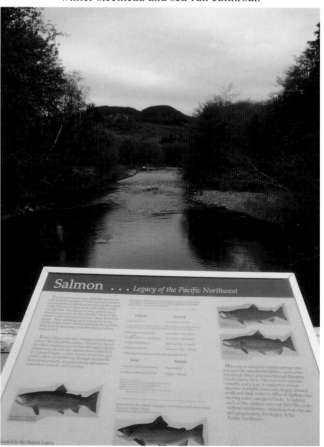

Steelhead. That's the name of the game in Oregon's southwest corner. The Rogue and North Umpqua, two of the most storied rivers in all of steelhead fly angling, carve monumental passage through the steep mountains of southwest Oregon. Both are tremendous river systems, draining substantial territories. The steelhead—winter- and summer-run fish—arrive in surprising numbers, given the history of rampant logging and mining on the steep-sided canyons through which these spectacular streams flow.

Although the Rogue and North Umpqua are barely two hours apart, many anglers are content to know only one of these magnificent streams: A lifetime could be spent unlocking the secrets of one or the other, let alone both rivers. Their relative proximity today is a result of modern roads and modern automobiles; only a few decades ago, the Rogue and North Umpqua might as well have been worlds apart as a journey from one to the other required substantial and taxing effort.

The highway leading up the North Umpqua was not completed until the middle of this century and only then so loggers could get at the green gold that carpeted the lush and rugged Cascade Range. Though the North Umpqua long remained inaccessible, it could hardly compare to the Rogue, whose precipitous canyons are to this day only barely negotiated by road. A generation of brave, adventurous oarsmen pioneered the Rogue's Middle and Lower reaches during the 1920s and 30s and by a dose of foresight, one long section of the Lower Rogue remains locked within a roadless canyon, accessible by boat and foot, but not by car.

While the legendary Rogue and North Umpqua rivers dominate the steelhead fly-angling scene of Southern Oregon, several lesser-known rivers offer significant runs of wild winter steelhead. Two of these are Rogue River tributaries (The Illinois and Applegate rivers); several others negotiate steep, twisting paths through the coast mountains before surrendering to the Pacific along the southwest coast. Among them are the Elk, Coquille, Pistol and Chetco.

Winter steelhead angling on the small coast streams is a hit-and-miss proposition: If you are traveling to the south coast from other locales, you had better keep an open mind. If one stream is blown out or running a little higher than is desirable, try the next river. All of the steelhead streams along the south coast, from the forks of the Coquille south of Coos Bay down to the Chetco and Winchuck near Brookings, are located within a fairly easy drive from one another, so flexibility in your choice of waters will help dramatically in hooking a winter steelhead from any of these attractive little rivers. Also consider that winter steelhead enter almost all of the small creeks on the south coast and many of these clear dramatically faster than the rivers.

Trout-angling may take a back seat to steelheading in southwestern Oregon, but that is not to say the region is devoid of quality fisheries for rainbow, brook and cutthroat trout. The Cascade Range of Southern Oregon offers many productive lakes while the headwater regions of many coastal streams provide excellent opportunities for small native cutthroat in intimate quarters. In fact, the catch-and-release trout rules implemented in 1996 for all coastal streams should create an excellent opportunity for quality cutthroat angling on countless tributaries and trunk streams up and down the coast. This is assuming the regulation can withstand a bombardment of pressure from the meat-hunting crowds who care little about the resource but who loath the fact that they can't fill a creel or freezer with hatchery or wild trout.

Fortunately, the Southwest Zone lacks a city of any size. Along the I5 corridor lie Roseburg, Grants Pass, Medford and Ashland, all reasonably quiet communities with plenty of personality. On the coast, Coos Bay is the largest of several prominent small towns, the others including Gold Beach, Bandon, Port Orford and Brookings. The south coast, especially from Port Orford down to Brookings, is Oregon's coastal banana belt: winter temperatures frequently climb 10 or 15 degrees above those registered on the central and north coast.

The Southern Oregon coast offers ample opportunity for inshore saltwater fly fishing. Redtail surfperch inhabit the sandy beaches and rockfish abound along the jetties. Calm summer surf even allows for casting flies along the rocky shoreline for greenling, cabezon, striped perch and rockfish. We can only hope that the relative isolation of the south coast will protect its striking beauty from the rampant development underway on Oregon's central and north coast.

The beautiful North Umpqua offers challenging fishing and challenging wading.

North Umpqua River

The legendary North Umpqua begins its storied journey high in the Cascades near Mt. Thielson, gathering the flows of many small rivulets before becoming one of the great steelhead rivers of enduring fame. Hard-won and always contested in various quarters, the 31-mile fly-only section on this scenic river has traditionally offered something of a haven to both steelhead and steelhead fly angler alike.

At the heart of the "fly water" is the mile or so of river near Steamboat Creek, a series of spectacular pools collectively termed the Camp Water. Major Mott, then Zane Grey, then Clarence Gordon all had their camps near here and it was Gordon who started a lodge on the south bank which eventually evolved into the Steamboat Inn of today, renowned for its elegant accommodations and fine dining.

In many ways, the North Umpqua is all steelhead rivers: As it gouges a path through steep canyon walls, the North Umpqua creates every imaginable kind of steelhead water and all of it in abundance. From glass-smooth tailouts and choppy runs, to gliding bedrock-rimmed chutes and deep pocket water, the North Umpqua offers something for everyone and in doing so becomes unique unto itself.

The magnitude of the river is impressive, not so much for the miles set aside for fly fishing, but for the countless steelhead lies found through this section and for the diversity of their natures. In one place you scramble down the steepest of inclines, picking your way through riprap and blackberries, always just one step away from getting to the bottom much more quickly than anticipated. When you finally emerge at the river's edge, you find all your efforts will yield but a single casting station—a solitary rock scarred with cleat marks from seasons past.

A handful of casts might cover this pool and then you are left with the prospect of renegotiating the highway embankment. The next pool offers stark contrast: You park alongside the highway on a gravel pullout and follow a well-worn path through a canopy of maples and Douglas firs to reach a sprawling pool whose cobblestone bottom is entirely wadeable from top to tailout. An hour and dozens of casts pass before you have entirely covered this elegant pool.

The North Umpqua is renowned for its treacherous wading, but an angler could spend an entire season fishing just those pools where sure footing is abundant; conversely, one could spend that same season negotiating pools where a thorough dunking is nearly as sure as the morning sun. In fact, I often think one ought to just sit down in the river first thing in the morning just to get it over with.

The fly water begins at the angling deadline about a half mile downstream from Soda Springs Dam. Here the river is characterized by a steep gradient and tumbling pocket water. Lightly fished, this upper end of the fly water is accessed by either Boulder Creek Trail or by a Forest Service spur that crosses the river just below the dam on a precarious little bridge. A number of steelhead negotiate this upper section of the fly water and some are taken each season; most of the fish—summer steelhead and especially winter steelhead—end their upriver journeys short of Soda Springs Dam.

A couple miles below the dam, Boulder Flat Campground and Eagle Rock Campground offer access to a handful of steelhead pools and runs. Following Hwy. 138 downstream from Eagle Rock Campground, you cross the river at Marster's Bridge. During the fall, chinook salmon can be observed on their spawning beds along the edges of the wide gravel flat around the corner from the bridge.

Forest Service Road Size 4770 heads off to the south just above Marster's Bridge, and a short distance up this gravel road lies the uppermost trailhead for the trail system (Mott Trail) that follows the river's south bank. Anglers willing to hike this trail can fish pools not accessible from the highway side of the river.

From Marster's Bridge to Dry Creek, anglers can access the river from either the trail on the south bank or from the highway, now on the north bank. Below Dry Creek, some of the more productive pools require a laborious (and at times treacherous) plunge over a long, steep grade off the highway embankment. Just over a mile below Dry Creek, the river sweeps through a long bend, hence the name of Horseshoe Bend campground.

Between Horseshoe Bend and Apple Creek campgrounds, some three miles of river are characterized by a steep climb down to water's edge and widely varied steelhead runs. Above Horseshoe Bend, the North Umpqua's gradient lessens some, and long, wadeable pools become more prevalent. Mott Trail follows the south bank through most of the fly water and, in a few instances, can provide access to pools and runs that are difficult, if not impossible, to fish from the highway side.

North Umpqua.

KEN MORRISH PHOTO

Some sections of this trail hang precipitously from the canyon wall and leave little if any access to the river below. This is especially true downstream from the Camp Water. Nonetheless, the Mott Trail allows more adventurous anglers to escape the crowds that often accumulate along the highway.

About four miles below Apple Creek, just around the corner from Island Campground, Mott Bridge crosses high over the river a short distance upstream from Steamboat Creek. Anglers can park just across the bridge and follow a short section of the Mott Trail that leads to the famed Camp Water.

So named because of its proximity to Mott's Camp (later Clarence Gordon's North Umpqua Lodge) that once stood on the south bank, the Camp Water is comprised of a number of revered, well-known steelhead pools. At the top, just below Mott Bridge, is the Bridge Hole. From atop the bridge, one can often spot steelhead holding in the channel between reefs of ledgerock. Below the Bridge Hole, the main current flows through a chute bordered on both sides by sheer ledges. This long, narrow glide is called Sawtooth, its name deriving from a section of sharp-edged, jagged reef that is famed for its ability to separate a steelhead from the angler on the other end.

Just below Sawtooth is Hayden's Run. Toward the highway side and just above the confluence of Steamboat Creek is Sweetheart, followed by the Confluence Hole and then the Station Hole. The latter, named for the Forest Service station that once stood atop the bank, was also called the Plank Pool because of a wooden platform that was built out over the water enabling anglers to position themselves for an easy time of it fishing this gliding, reef-bound run.

Below Station, the river surges through a short rapids before fanning out into the most magnificent of steelhead pools, this one known as the Boat Hole. Upper Boat (or Top of the Boat) is a narrow chute above the main pool; Middle Boat and Lower Boat sprawl out over a tremendous cobblestone bar, studded here and there with bedrock reefs.

Major Jordan Lawrence Mott, who set up the first camp on the river's south bank in 1929, hired Zeke Allen, a local guide, as his cook and assistant at the fly-fishing camp that first year. Visitors would signal the camp via a bell on the north bank and Allen would then ferry them across on a rowboat, hence the pool's name.

At its lower reaches, the Boat Hole tails into a narrowing chute of bedrock reefs, forming the Kitchen Pool, so named because it was overlooked by Mott's kitchen tent. Later, a trail led from Clarence Gordon's dining hall down the bank to the Kitchen Pool. Below Kitchen, the flow glides through a series of ledge-rock pools: The Fighting Hole, Upper, Middle and Lower Mott, Glory Hole and Gordon.

From the Bridge Hole to Gordon and beyond, the flow glides over and through ledgerock reefs and channels, forming what Trey Combs called "the most celebrated waters in all of steelhead fly fishing." (Combs, *Steelhead Fly Fishing*, 1991).

These storied pools continue around the next bend, below Steamboat Inn: Maple Ridge, Jeannie, Abernathy, Takahashi (named for Zane Grey's Japanese cook, George Takahashi), Knouse. Further downstream one finds the Ledges, Tree Pool, Divide Pool, Williams Creek Riffle, the Log Hole and Discovery Pool. The popular Archie, a deep reef-bound tailout, lies some half a mile downstream from the Discovery Pool, with ample fishable water in between. Another mile or so downriver is Bogus Creek Campground and from there to the lower boundary of the fly water (about 12 miles), the Umpqua offers countless pools and runs where steelhead lie during both the summer and winter seasons.

The popular pools are easy to find: Look for pullouts along the highway. These same pools generally feature the same worn path of rocks scarred from wading cleats. Hence if you find yourself wondering which rock is *the* casting station, just look for the one decorated with cleat scars.

Throughout the North Umpqua (and especially from Apple Creek to the lower end of the fly water) dry-fly anglers will find a number of perfectly smooth tailouts where a skating fly might bring an explosive boil first thing in the morning or at last light—maybe any time of day when the river is uncrowded.

Summer or winter, steelhead return to these pools each season. And each of these revered pools offers something new and different, from the narrow curling chute at the Confluence Hole to the sprawling breadth of the Boat Hole, to the deep green channels of the Mott Pool.

Even in all their classic resplendence, the pools comprising the Camp Water only hint at the full magnitude of the North Umpqua's fly-only section. For miles below and miles above the Steamboat area, the North Umpqua gouges a course through solid bedrock, cascading through a deep canyon and offering fly anglers the opportunity to cast elegant steelhead flies over the most diverse of watery terrain: In one pool you are confined to a single large rock, from which you will lengthen your line some four or five feet on each successive cast until your fly has covered the sweet part of the pool; immediately below you find a classic, wadeable pool where each cast steers a course through new waters, where a steelhead might be forthcoming on the first short cast at the pool's head or the last offering deep into the tailout.

In many places, your backcast must dart expertly through the understory of maple and alders; in other pools you must elevate the backstroke to clear the highway embankment immediately behind. Round the next bend, however, and you find a run where the cast can blossom to its full grace and elegance with no obstacles to steer its course. Here you stand high above the water and cast a hundred feet; there you wade in behind a boulder and dabble a ten-foot cast. In many ways, the North Umpqua is all steelhead rivers wrapped into one and in that sense, this graceful and challenging river cannot help but prepare you for other streams in other places.

Fishing the Summer Run

By June, summer steelhead begin to accumulate in the lower reaches of the fly-water section and by mid-July, they are present in numbers that attract attention from anglers. The peak of the run occurs during August and fishing remains productive through September and October.

During this time frame, however, the weather pattern changes from the unpredictable nature of early summer to the hot days of July and August, to the increasing clouds and autumn cooling of October. The high water might roar through the river's canyon through June only to dwindle to a comparative trickle by August. During late summer, in fact, the North Umpqua sometimes runs low enough that the water warms to the point where steelhead and steelhead anglers alike will find things rather unpleasant.

During these periods of low, warm water, steelhead often act sulky and seem disinclined to move for the fly. At the same time, anglers discard the waders in exchange for shorts, heavy socks and the usual cleated boots. The fish can still be had, however, by those who fish the early morning and late evening hours and who spend the mid-afternoon casting over the river's many shaded pools and runs.

Indeed, despite the occasional bouts with low, warm water, August remains the most popular month on the North Umpqua. Vacationers from afar can set up camp at any of numerous campgrounds; locals try to hide from them, fishing out-of-the-way places and fishing popular pools early and late in the day and mid-week.

By late August, the North Umpqua can be a busy river at times, especially for those who stick to the Camp Water in the vicinity of Steamboat. Arrive a month previous, however, and one might cast over empty pools and untouched tailouts during the pleasant mornings and quiet evenings of mid-week July days.

The fishing holds up through the early and mid-fall, with September and early October being decidedly pleasant and colorful times on the river. The maples adorn themselves in their full autumn regalia of yellows, golds, oranges and reds, offering poetic contrast to the steep canyon walls cloaked in the dark green of firs, cedars, pines and hemlock.

The North Umpqua's summer steelhead are a remarkable strain of fish. They habitually use the river's bedrock reefs to separate themselves from attached fly anglers. Fish of seven and eight pounds are common; 10- to 15-pound steelhead are present in reasonable numbers and a handful of 20-pound bruisers cross the ladders at Winchester Dam each summer.

Some 75 to 80 percent of these fish are of hatchery origin and can be identified as such by their fin clips. These hatchery fish, however, come entirely from North Umpqua brood stock: The Oregon Department of Fish and Wildlife traps steelhead at Rock Creek and milks these fish to raise the smolts that will be returned to the river at about eight inches in length. Brood-stock steelhead are selected more-or-less at random to assure genetic diversity and they are accumulated throughout the summer run in an effort to assure diversity in the timing of future returns.

Traditional steelhead wet flies will serve you well on the North Umpqua. Among the more popular patterns are the following: Skunks, Green-Butt Skunk, Black Gordon, Purple Peril, Umpqua Special, Cumming's Special, Brad's Brat, Steelhead Muddler (wet) and others. For what it's worth, my personal favorites are the Spawning Purple, Maxwell's Purple Matuka, Skunk and Brad's Brat. Skating flies are popular for fishing the river's smooth glides and tailouts. Some favorites include Bombers, Dry Muddlers, October Caddis and stonefly patterns. Every once in a while, a steelhead is taken on a dead-drift dry fly, especially late in the season when the big orange *Dicosmoecus* caddis (October caddis) are in abundance.

Lastly, North Umpqua anglers should choose their wading gear with foresight: Cleated boots or sandals are a must. During the hottest part of summer, one might opt for shorts or long pants instead of waders; during the fall, neoprenes will fight the chill of early morning and evening. Either way—and it bears repeating—cleated soles are mandatory.

Fishing the Winter Run

A few winter steelhead often find their way up the North Umpqua by December; still more during January. February through early April, however, offers the bulk of the winter run and consequently provides the best fishing.

These North Umpqua winter steelhead average substantially larger than their summer brethren. Twelve to 15-pound fish are common and a few fish approaching and exceeding 20 pounds are taken each season (most of these by terminal-gear anglers fishing downstream from the fly-only section).

The typical North Umpqua winter run will exceed 5,000 fish, all of them wild North Umpqua stock. Half or less of the winter steelhead will ultimately spawn in the Steamboat/Canton Creek system and as many as 20 percent of the total may end up spawning in tributaries (and in the main river) as far upstream as Soda Springs Dam. Still more fish will use streams below Steamboat, including Rock Creek. Most spawning activity among winter steelhead occurs in April and May—several weeks later than the summer steelhead.

Throughout most of the winter season, the North Umpqua will run higher and less clear than during the summer and fall. Still, most winters offer ample opportunity to fish during reasonably low and clear flows. Heavy rains any time during the winter or unusually warm weather that causes massive snow-melt will swell the river rapidly; these heavy flows typically subside in one to three days when more stable conditions return.

Often the river above the Camp Water will run quite clear only to have Steamboat Creek discolor the lower section with a glacial-green flow. Even at high water, however, those who know the river well will find places to fish.

Traditionally, the winter season on the fly-section has gone more-or-less unnoticed by the vast majority of fly anglers. Things are changing now. Each winter greets increasing numbers of anglers bent on trying their luck with the river's wild winter steelhead. Still, a crowded winter day rarely compares to a crowded summer day. Those who fish the winter run often do so under less-than-perfect conditions. The North Umpqua drainage gets ample precipitation, much of it in the form of rainfall. Along with the usual cleated boots, a rain parka should be close at hand during a winter-time trip to the North Umpqua.

The same eight- and nine-weight rods that serve so well during the summer are perfectly suited to winter fishing. Some kind of sinking-line system will help keep the fly deep in the swollen winter flows. My preference is for a shooting taper system. Usually I opt for a Cortland Type VI sinking head attached to monofilament running line. In the deepest pools I might switch to a heavier head, perhaps a section of 400-grain fly line. A short leader (3 to 5 feet) is well-suited to these fast-sinking heads.

Other anglers might opt for high-density sink-tip fly lines like those designed by Jim Teeny, McKenzie Fly Tackle Company, as well as the other major line manufacturers. These lines will certainly fish the fly deep, but for me at least, they are more laborious to cast than the head systems.

Many of the North Umpqua's ledge-rock pools are more effectively fished with a weighted pattern. Joe Howell relies on Comet-style flies for some of his high-water fishing and he fishes these flies on a ten-foot sink-tip line. With this set-up, he is able to sink a fly quickly in narrow slots where a typical quartering cast proves rather inefficient. Unlike sinking heads, the sink-tip line allows for roll casting, thus opening up just about any kind of water to effective fly fishing.

Those who prefer unweighted flies are confined to certain water types. Luckily, however, the North Umpqua boasts every conceivable kind of water and all of it in abundance.

The patterns used for summer fishing work just as well during the winter, although colored water often begs for larger sizes. Some anglers, myself included, often fish Spey-style steelhead patterns during the winter, with the typical shades of orange, black, purple and hot pink being productive. Sizes range from 2 to as large as 4/0 and heavy-wire hooks will help keep the fly down during the drift and swing.

Flies of the North Umpqua

As one would expect, a history of this legendary river would include the origination of numerous patterns dressed specifically for the North Umpqua. Indeed this is the case: Generations of anglers have created numerous North Umpqua dressings, some of which have become standards not only on this river but on steelhead waters everywhere.

I am indebted to Trey Combs—as are we all—for his diligent work in compiling historical data on countless steelhead patterns. His book *Steelhead Fly Fishing and Flies* (Frank Amato Publications, 1976) includes the origins of virtually all the popular steelhead dressings and a great many lesser-known ones. Combs' subsequent book, *Steelhead Fly Fishing* (Lyons & Burford, 1991), likewise includes interesting historical information about the origination of many steelhead patterns.

Of all the dressings originated on the North Umpqua, none is more widely recognized than the Skunk. No doubt a product of several regions, the Skunk is so simple in its design that it would be surprising if only one tier were responsible for its conception. Another widely recognized North Umpqua pattern is the Golden Demon, which Zane Grey brought from New Zealand to Southern Oregon in the early 1930s. Not a fly of Northwest origins, the Golden Demon nonetheless remains popular long after Zane Grey's last days fishing the North Umpqua and Rogue rivers.

Zane Grey's guide Joe DeBernardi (perhaps with Grey's input) may have created the well-known and long-popular Umpqua Special. Exact origins are unknown. Nonetheless, the elegant Umpqua Special remains a popular fly.

Clarence Gordon created a number of flies for his beloved river, the most popular today being the Black Gordon. The Grey Gordon and the Orange Gordon are more-or-less lost to modern steelheading but are still productive and well-conceived dressings. Gordon and Umpqua guide (at the time) Ward Cummings devised the Cummings or Cummings Special during the 1930s. Today it is a steelheading standard, though not so widely known as the Black Gordon.

Other, little-known patterns developed on the North Umpqua include the lovely Stevenson Special, devised by C.N. Stevenson in the 1940s and the Surveyor, essentially a variation on the Umpqua Special that was no doubt named after the Surveyor Hole upstream from Mott Bridge.

Today, Joe Howell, owner of Blue Heron Fly Shop just across the highway from the river above Idleyld Park, sets the standard for North Umpqua steelhead flies. Several of his creations will be tied by future generations and will take steelhead on the North Umpqua for decades to come.

Joe is especially known for his dry steelhead patterns and for his elegant Spey-style dressings. His Coon Muddler and Flat-head Muddler have become favorites with North Umpqua dry-fly enthusiasts.

Skunk

Tag: Silver
Tail: Red hackle fibers
Body: Black chenille, wool or similar
Rib: Silver tinsel
Throat: Black hackle
Wing: White hair

Umpqua Special

Tail: White hair (bucktail, calf tail, polar bear)
Body: Rear third yellow wool, front 2/3 red wool or chenille
Rib: Silver tinsel
Throat: Brown hackle
Wing: White hair with sparse bunches of red hair on either side
Cheeks: Jungle cock

Black Gordon

Body: Rear third red wool, front 2/3 black wool or similar
Rib: Gold oval
Throat: Black hackle
Wing: Black bear or similar

Cummings Special

Body: Rear third yellow silk or floss, front 2/3 claret wool
Rib: Silver tinsel
Throat: Claret hackle
Wing: Brown bucktail or similar
Cheeks: Jungle cock

Silver Admiral (Polly Rosborough)

Hook: Wright & McGill 1197N or similar
Tail: Fluorescent hot pink hackle fibers
Body: Fluorescent hot pink wool yarn
Rib: Flat silver tinsel
Hackle: Fluorescent hot pink
Wing: White bucktail or calf tail

North Umpqua Logistics

Eugene is about two hours from the fly water, Portland, about 4 1/2 hours. From the town of Roseburg, Highway 138 departs Interstate 5 and reaches the North Umpqua at the little community of Glide. From there, the highway parallels the river virtually all the way up the fly water.

From the east side of the Cascade Mountains, Highway 97, the main north-south route in Central Oregon, connects with Hwy. 138 about 75 miles south of Bend and about 65 miles north of Klamath Falls. After departing Hwy. 97 at Diamond Lake Junction, Hwy. 138 traverses the Cascades, reaching an elevation of almost 6,000 feet at the top of the pass. The drive from Bend takes about three hours.

If you travel this route from Central Oregon to the North Umpqua during winter, be prepared for winter storms. I've hit blizzards in late April. The route from Roseburg is more tame, owing to its low elevation. However, Highway 138, especially from Glide eastward, is replete with log trucks all year and has narrow, winding curves and nasty potholes. Anglers should strive to keep one eye on the road while the other longs for the river below.

Visitors to the North Umpqua can find accommodations ranging from the most rudimentary of fishing camps to the most well-appointed lodging. The latter is available at Steamboat Inn, located just downstream from the famous Camp Water on the highway side of the river.

The Forest Service and the BLM operate campgrounds all along the river. Most open during May, although several (Boulder Flat, Apple Creek, Island, Steamboat Falls, Williams Creek) remain open during the winter. A $10 bill will buy you a night's stay at the campgrounds, but be forewarned: Camp space can be hard to come by on a weekend during the heart of the summer season.

Glide and Idleyld Park, downstream from the lower boundary of the fly water, offer enough services to get you by, including gas, food, drink, some lodging and post offices. Toward the upper end of the fly water, the store at Dry Creek includes a gas pump and a concrete floor that will tolerate your wading spikes if you stop in for a mid-morning or mid-evening cup of coffee.

Guide services can be arranged through Joe Howell at the Blue Heron Fly Shop. While Joe himself no longer guides, he can suggest a competent guide for you.

Blue Heron Fly Shop
HC-60 Box 8-B
Idleyld Park, OR 97447
503/496-0448

A Question of Etiquette

Imagine wading into the top of a steelhead run, intent on fishing through, only to have an angler step into the tailout without first asking? The only thing that could make matters worse would be to have that angler stand in one spot, ruining your opportunity to fish out the pool. Similarly, imagine walking the trail to a favorite run only to find an angler already standing in the middle of the pool. You sit on a rock to wait your turn, but soon realize the other fellow is not moving. Steelhead fly-fishing etiquette be damned.

This age of increasing pressures on our outdoor resources dictates more than ever that fly anglers recognize and practice time-honored and time-tested river etiquette. Foremost among steelhead fly-fishing rules of behavior is the importance of moving through a pool. I am reminded of the old writers who sought to educate their readers on the importance of etiquette and on the importance of pursuing their art in a gentlemanly manner (no sexism intended). Today's body of contemporary literature seeks to inform. Give them the information they need to catch fish and you will sell articles and books. The goal of the majority of today's writing is to tell anglers how to catch more and bigger fish; it is the rare piece that tells them how to do so in a gentlemanly manner. Perhaps Claude Krieder said it best in his 1948 book titled *Steelhead:*

> Sporting ethics entail consideration of other anglers in these days of heavily fished waters, and there is a certain code that properly applies where many anglers gather on a popular pool or riffle. The casters should start toward the head of the water and work through in turn, each angler following the next and a decent interval behind. Thus each has an opportunity to test his skills the entire length of the pool, and no man may appropriate any one spot as his own without soon learning by hint—or plain forcible language—that he is not playing the game.

Indeed, these very concepts in steelheading etiquette are spelled out on a sign at the parking area above the Camp Water near Mott Bridge, yet they are ignored by a small but highly visible minority who seem to prefer hooking lots of fish by whatever means necessary than to hook a few fish in a gentlemanly manner. As I've told people, shooting ducks on the water is awfully effective, but that doesn't make it sporting.

Those of us who practice traditional steelheading etiquette can be our own best friends by going out of our way to promote the classic steelheading techniques and their inherent set of codes. Indeed, I would suggest that we are under something of an obligation to do so—a view that I think will hold increasingly more merit as the number of anglers increases on the North Umpqua and our other prized Northwest steelhead rivers.

Rogue River

The Rogue River's fame and stature as a Northwest steelhead river can only be rivaled by its neighbor, the North Umpqua. The Rogue River was among the first steelhead streams to become nationally renowned among fly anglers, largely due to the writings of the river's most famous angler, Zane Grey, who first visited the Rogue during the 1920s. He brought with him a fly whose fame rivals that of the river where it was first baptized for steelhead—the Golden Demon.

The Rogue's physical stature is somewhat overwhelming. It gathers its headwaters high in the Cascades from Diamond Lake and from numerous rivulets draining the high country west of Crater Lake. The Rogue has gained respectable size by the time it reaches Lost Creek Reservoir, one of several impoundments along the river. Below Lost Creek Dam, the river flows through a mile-long tailwater termed the Holly Water by local fly anglers. Rainbow and brown trout to several pounds inhabit this reach, whose physical characteristics are little more than those of a shallow, glorified canal. Nonetheless, these are rich waters flowing from the dam and rooted weed beds provide good habitat

A typical Rogue River "half-pounder" spans 14 to 18 inches.

for myriad mayflies and caddis; even giant stoneflies hatch on the riffle sections above and below.

The Holy Water is easily accessed from a nice park located above its banks. Follow Hwy. 62 from the west (Medford) or from the east (Diamond Lake Junction). The highway crosses the Rogue a couple miles below Lost Creek Reservoir, and on the north side of the bridge a well-marked road leads up to the hatchery and dam. Drive up to the hatchery diversion dam and turn right, crossing the river adjacent to the holding ponds. The Holy Water is now on your right. Continue toward the hatchery and then turn left to reach the parking areas.

Downstream from the Holy Water, the Rogue is closed to fishing for a short distance adjacent to the hatchery. Below the deadline, the Upper Rogue fishery begins, its primary fly-rod attraction being a substantial run of adult summer steelhead that begin to arrive early to midsummer. From the hatchery down to Shady Cove—a reach of about 12 miles—the Rogue is paralleled by Hwy. 62, which offers fair to good access for bank anglers. Still a drift boat offers the distinct advantage of allowing anglers to float between good fly-water runs and then wade the best sections.

The uppermost launch (McGregor Park) is located at the hatchery downstream from Lost Creek Dam. The McGregor Park launch is a nice concrete ramp which should eliminate any thought of rough-launching a short distance downstream at the highway bridge. The next ramp is located at Casey Park, only a mile-and-a-half downstream, but the McGregor Park drift allows you to fish some nice fly water located on the elbow bend downstream from the hatchery deadline.

Rogue Elk Park is the next launch, located less than three miles downstream from Casey Park, also along Hwy. 62. Shady Cove Park offers the next ramp, some five miles downstream of Rogue Elk Park. Drift boat anglers can thus chose any of three different upriver launches to make the drift down to Shady Cove or they can float shorter lengths, say from McGregor down to Rogue Elk Park, to maximize fishing time during the day. Another option is to float from Shady Cove (or points upriver) down to Takelma or Dodge Bridge, both located off Rogue River Drive. The latter ramp is located just off Hwy. 234, which turns west off Hwy. 62 about six miles south of Shady Cove. Takelma is situated about three miles north of the bridge.

The river below Dodge Bridge offers some good prospects for fly anglers, but its rapids (which should be scouted before being negotiated) should only be attempted by experienced oarsmen. A 10-mile drift from Dodge Bridge down to Touvelle State Park covers this reach and includes a plunge through a nasty piece of white-water called Rattlesnake. Touvelle Park is located two miles northwest of White City on Table Rock Road. From Hwy. 62, turn west on Antelope Road at White City and then north on Table Rock Road. From the south, take Table Rock Road out of Medford or follow Hwy. 62 up to E. Vilas Road or Antelope Road and turn west to reach Table Rock Road.

Below Gold Ray Dam, the Upper Rogue continues, flowing along Interstate-5, through the town of Rogue River and through yet another impoundment, Savage Rapids Dam. Below Savage Rapids, the so-called Middle Rogue begins, paralleling the interstate westward a few miles to Grants Pass. The reach between the dam and Grants Pass offers some good steelhead water for drift boat anglers, but little in the way of bank access except at the parks. The first launch is at Gold Hill (Gold Nugget Park), off Hwy. 234. From here you can drift down to Valley of the Rogue Park, located off I5 about three miles southeast of Rogue River. A third ramp is located in the town of Rogue River at Coyote Evans Wayside.

The entire Upper Rogue, from the Gold Ray Pool up to Lost Creek Dam, offers good fishing for an early summer run of adult summer steelhead, most of them of hatchery origin. Because the run peaks between mid-June and mid-July, high-water years can limit the fishing. Low-water years make for ideal fly-fishing conditions on the upper river.

The Middle Rogue extends downstream through Grants Pass and Galice to the end of the road at Grave Creek. This 50-plus-mile reach is the most heavily fished section by fly anglers seeking the river's famed half-pounders. The half-pounders are small summer steelhead, less than 20 inches in length, that return to the river after only a few months in salt water.

Most steelhead spend one to three years in salt water before returning to their natal rivers; half-pounders spend less than a year and thus arrive sexually immature and incapable of spawning. Like any other steelhead, they grow to eight or nine inches in the river and then heed the call of the far-away Pacific. Their life at sea is brief by steelhead standards, for the smolts that exit the river in late spring return that very fall, mostly in October, having attained a modest length of 12 to 16 inches, sometimes a bit more. These half-pounders then over-winter in the river and again head for the salt the following spring. Upon their next return, they will be mature fish, ready to spawn that winter, and will span 16 to 20 inches or more. The occasional six- to 10-pound steelhead is likely a repeat spawner (a half-pounder making its second spawning run) although a few actual two- and three-salt summer steelhead ascend the river each fall.

Don't let their size fool you. The half-pounders have enough salt under their belts to fight a lot like their older brethren. They just don't pack as much weight with which to back up their hell-bent-for-leather attitude toward being stuck in the jaw with a steelhead fly. They do offer some advantages over full-sized steelhead. First they feed more actively in fresh water than regular steelhead, making the half-pounders an aggressive bunch when it comes to chasing a swinging fly fished on a floating or sink-tip line. Second, they arrive and hold in pods or schools, so hook one fish and you're likely to hook several, maybe even a bunch. On a good day, with a good guide, you may well hook two or three dozen half-pounders from 12 to 20 inches and an occasional repeat spawner of six to 10 pounds.

If you've never fished the Rogue, hire one of the established guides. The experience alone will justify the cost, but perhaps more significantly, a guide like Ray Slusser will cut down your learning curve considerably. The Rogue is tough on newcomers; she makes you work hard to uncover her secrets. If you have lots of time on your hands, then dive right in; if you want to maximize your fish-catching time or short-cut the learning curve, spring for a guide.

If you're going at it sans guide, the Middle Rogue offers several great floats for newcomers: 1. Valley of the Rogue Park to the town of Rogue River runs along I5 and covers an easy four miles. You can do this one twice a day if you wish, once in the morning and again in the after-noon/evening. 2. Lathrop Landing to Whitehorse Park covers about six miles just west of Grants Pass (access from Upper River Road). 3. Whitehorse Park to Robberson Bridge is an eight-mile float and is also accessed via Upper River Road. 4. Robberson Bridge to Hog Creek Landing covers five miles, with the take-out located off Merlin-Galice Road about seven miles west of Merlin. Each of these four drifts will keep you away from the heavy Class II, III and IV rapids for which the Rogue is famed.

Shuttle service can be arranged locally at a variety of places, including the tackle shops, Galice Resort or Little Pantry in Merlin. Lodging along the Middle Rogue includes campgrounds at Alameda Bar (north of Galice), Indian Mary (east of Galice), Griffin Park, Whitehorse Park and Schroeder Park (all west of Grants Pass) and at Valley of the Rogue Park (east of Rogue River on I5). Motels abound in Grants Pass and the surrounding area, and high-class riverside accommodations are available at places such as Morrison's Lodge and Galice Resort (the former employs its own staff of qualified guides).

On both the Middle and Lower Rogue, steelhead guides earn their money the old-fashioned way. Legendary Rogue oarsman Glen Wooldridge proved as much decades ago when he dynamited the boulder-strewn rapids at Blossom Bar to create safe passage for generations of floaters to come. In many ways Wooldridge pioneered the Rogue, in 1915 he was among the first to float the notoriously wild river and in 1947 completing what was thought to be an insane undertaking at the time: motoring nearly 100 miles up the wild Rogue River Canyon from the river's mouth at Gold Beach to the town of Grants Pass.

During the Wooldridge era, a time when the river's noted angling guests included the likes of Zane Grey and Ginger Rogers, Rogue guides pioneered unique new methods of pursuing the abundant summer steelhead. Then, even more so than now, the Rogue was a floater's fishery: Steep canyon walls, sheer bedrock reefs and escarpments, and numerous unwadeable yet productive pools dictated a departure from the familiar steelhead/Atlantic salmon pattern of wading a run from top to bottom and quartering casts down and across.

The adjustment made by Rogue guides was a simple one, at least in principle: Make the boat do the work. In other words, steelhead guides

The stunning Middle Rogue offers many classic, wadable steelhead runs.

all of the parks and launches along the river offer good foot access to highly productive steelhead water, but for fear of loosing my hide at the hands of the local fly-angling club, I'll leave the other walk-in access sites for you to discover through your own explorations. Despite some good walk-in access at certain places, though, the Middle Rogue is better fished by drift boat.

Those familiar with the river and/or with advanced boating skills, have several additional float options, including the run through spectacular Hells Gate Canyon. Seven ramps are located below Hell's Gate Canyon. The first is Indian Mary, a couple miles downstream; the second is Ennis Riffle, another two miles downstream and the third is Galice Boat Landing, at the little town of Galice (these three are county accesses with cement ramps). Rand Access is a BLM site a couple miles below Galice and is followed by the county's Alameda Bar at Alameda County Park. The last ramp before the final take-out at Grave Creek is at Argo Riffle, another BLM site featuring a gravel launch. Grave Creek, the final exit before the lengthy and roadless canyon drift, lies just below the Galice Road Bridge, which crosses high over the river.

The Lower Rogue begins at Grave Creek and extends 60 miles down to the mouth at Gold Beach. A roadless reach at the top of this section begins at Grave Creek Landing and extends 35 miles down to Foster Bar. Jet sleds can access the lower end of this Wild and Scenic River, within the Wild Rogue Wilderness Area, but are not allowed past Blossom Bar. Most of this roadless reach is the domain of floaters, with splash-and-gigglers abundant both summer and fall.

If you decide to float the Lower Rogue's roadless section below Grave Creek, be sure to consult a good floater's guide, such as the *Handbook to the Rogue River Canyon*, by James M. Quinn, James W. Quinn and James G. King; 1978. Published by Educational Adventures, Inc., the book is available at many outdoor stores and through Frank Amato Publications. Another good book is *Oregon River Tours* by John Garren (Garren Publishing, 1991), which offers a very detailed chapter on the Grave Creek to Foster Bar trip.

Your best bet for fishing the Lower Rogue is to hire one of the fishing guides in the area and make a three- to five-day trip of it. Otherwise, during the summer season, you must obtain a permit, these being allocated on a lottery basis for non-commercial users. For information about obtaining a permit, contact the U.S. Forest Service Rand Information Center in Merlin (541/479-3735). A floater's guide is available from the forest service. The permit season ends in the fall (check with the Forest Service for the date) and at that time river-use often increases. In any event, the Rogue Canyon is no place for beginning boaters as it features one honest-to-God waterfall drop at Rainie Falls (a Class V rapids) and numerous Class IV, III and II rapids. Most drift-boaters line through the fish ladder at Rainie Falls, which eats its share of watercraft each season.

You can also hike into the roadless section on a good trail that runs along the north bank between Grave Creek and Foster Bar. In many places, the trail accesses excellent steelhead water. Grave Creek lies at the end of Galice Road, which leads downriver from the town of Merlin (north of Grants Pass off Interstate 5). Galice Road will cross the river twice, first below Hells Gate Canyon and then immediately above the well-signed access at Grave Creek (the ramp is across the bridge on the left). To reach the take-out at Foster Bar, drive upriver from Gold Beach to Agnus or take the long, circuitous journey over Bear Creek Road (Forest Primary Route 23) from Galice. A third route is the road down from Powers along the South Fork Coquille. Either one or both of the latter routes are subject to closure at any time due to adverse road conditions, leaving the Gold Beach route as your only option. From the south side of the bay at Gold Beach, turn east on a well-marked road (Curry County Route 595/Forest Route 33) and head east for about 35 miles, crossing first the Illinois River and then the Rogue above Agness.

The Rogue Canyon offers an abundance of excellent steelhead water, but don't expect to have much solitude: This has become one of Oregon's biggest splash-and-giggle playgrounds. Below the Wild and Scenic Rogue Canyon, you can fish by jet sled or drift boat, accessing lots of exceptional water that does not get the raft and kayak traffic associated

fished their clients from the back of solidly built wooden Rogue River drift boats (different in character from the far more familiar McKenzie-style drift boats in use throughout the West today). The client would cast downstream and across while the oarsman held position against the flow at the top end of a run or pool. Then the guide would back the boat slowly downstream, often oaring against surprisingly strong currents and frequently swinging the craft slowly side-to-side through the best slots. This way the angler still fished the fly on the ever-productive cross-current swing, covering a great deal of water, while the motion of the boat helped sweep the fly back and forth across the pool's most productive reaches.

With a skilled oarsman at the helm, an angler could fish an entire run with a single cast. Or, again because of the guide's skill in positioning and handling the boat, the angler could cast repeatedly, fishing the water in much the same way as if he or she were wading.

Either way the guide worked hard, which may explain why today so few Rogue guides practice the classic techniques developed on and for this special river. A few throwbacks still ply their craft with a studied reverence for the Rogue's storied past. Among the best is Ray Slusser, whose callused hands and work-hardened arms carry the torch of tradition for pioneering Rogue River fly-fishing guides of the past.

Bank access is only fair along the Middle Rogue and is limited primarily by the precipitous canyon through which the river flows. Almost

with the Grave Creek-to-Foster Bar reach. Contact Oregon Guides & Packers or local tackle shops for a current list of Lower Rogue guides and outfitters.

Moreover, much of the lower river, below Foster Bar, is road accessible although in places you will have to scramble down steep slopes to get to the water. The North Bank Rogue River Road accesses lots of good fly water along the lower 10 miles of the river. The turn-off is off the north side of the Hwy. 101 bridge at the river's mouth in Gold Beach. Boat ramps for the lower river are located as follows, starting upriver: 1. Cougar Lane Store (private, permission needed) about a mile east from Agness. 2. Lucas Beach, about a mile west from Agness. 3. Quosatana Campground, 15 miles east of Gold Beach. 4. Huntley Park, five miles east of Gold Beach and Ferry Ramp, four miles east of Gold Beach off North Bank Road.

The Lower Rogue also features a series of well-known backcountry lodges that cater to steelhead and salmon anglers. Among them are Black Bar Lodge (541/479-6504), Marial Lodge (541/479-4923), Half Moon Bar Lodge (541/247-6968), Paradise Lodge (541/247-6022). Also there is Morrison's Lodge a storied lodge on the Middle Rogue near Galice (541/476-3825).

Rogue River Steelhead Flies

Over the decades, the Rogue River and its steelhead fishery have inspired the creation of numerous patterns that have survived the test of time and many others of which only scant mention is made in the literature of today. Some of the river's enduring patterns were originated by some of the sport's most noted steelhead anglers, including Al Knudson, Mike Kennedy and Ike Tower to name just three. In addition to its own patterns, the Rogue also inspired a style of steelhead fly: "Rogue River" flies were frequently dressed on small, double hooks and crafted with upright and divided wings. The development of the "Rogue River style" steelhead fly paralleled to some extent the development of the Rogue's unique style of steelhead fishing from a drift boat. The double hook balanced the fly perfectly in the water while the upright wing caused the fly to dance in the currents. Many guides asked their clients to twitch the fly, causing it to further shimmer and flutter. By the late 1970s, however, double-hooked flies were beginning to fade and today they are used only sparingly, partly because of the damage they can cause a small half-pounder that is intended for release anyway, and partly because the art of tying on doubles has simply faded in recent years.

Rogue River expert Al Brunell tied the flies that appear here, and this list is representative of patterns that originated on the Rogue.

Rogue River Special

Tail:	Red hackle fibers
Butt:	Yellow wool
Body:	Red wool
Rib:	Silver tinsel
Wing:	White
Cheeks:	Jungle cock (optional)
Head:	Black with black-on-white painted eyes (optional)

Kennedy Rogue Red Ant (Mike Kennedy)

Tag:	Silver
Tail:	Red hackle fibers
Butt:	Peacock herl
Body:	Red wool (usually ribbed with fine gold oval)
Hackle:	Furnace
Wing:	Red fox squirrel tail

Juicy Bug (Ben Chandler/Ike Tower)

Hook:	Bronze or black double, size 6-8
Tag:	Gold or silver fine oval (optional)
Tail:	Red hackle fibers
Butt:	Black chenille
Body:	Red chenille
Rib:	Silver oval tinsel
Wing:	White bucktail or calf tail, upright and divided
Cheeks:	Jungle cock

Golden Demon

Tag:	Silver or gold tinsel
Tail:	Golden pheasant crest
Body:	Gold tinsel, embossed or flat with oval or wire rib
Hackle:	Orange
Wing:	Bronze mallard (according to sources written at the time Zane Grey first visited Oregon's Rogue River) or brown bucktail or similar

Blue Boy (Gene Rizzi)

Tail:	Red hackle fibers
Butt:	Red chenille
Body:	Blue chenille
Rib:	Silver
Hackle:	Light blue
Wing:	White

Yellow Fever (Gene Rizzi)

Tail:	Black hackle fibers
Butt:	Black chenille
Body:	Black chenille with yellow chenille pulled under
Hackle:	Black
Wing:	Yellow calf tail

Ginger Quill

Tail:	Ginger hackle fibers
Body:	Gray floss
Wing:	Brown bucktail or similar

Illahe Special

Tail:	Peacock sword
Butt:	Hot orange or burnt orange floss
Body:	Peacock herl
Hackle:	Soft grizzly, palmered through peacock herl
Wings:	Brown bucktail

Silver Ant (Ike Tower)

Tail:	Amherst pheasant tippet fibers
Butt:	Black chenille
Body:	Silver tinsel, embossed
Wings:	Gray squirrel

Royal Coachman Bucktail

Tail: Golden pheasant tippet fibers
Body: Peacock herl fore and aft, divided by red floss
Hackle: Brown
Wings: White bucktail

Witherwox

Tail: Teal flank feathers
Butt: Green chenille
Body: Red floss
Tag: Silver oval
Throat: Teal flank
Wings: White bucktail

Chaveney

Tail: Golden pheasant tippet fibers
Body: Gray wool
Rib: Silver oval
Wings: Brown bucktail or squirrel

Illinois River

The beautiful Illinois River has been designated a catch-and-release-only river for all species because of concern over declining runs, at least in part due to extensive allocation of water for agriculture, along with the typical story of rampant timber harvest and extensive mining. This includes its indigenous run of native winter steelhead along with its typically robust run of Rogue River half-pounders, which seek refuge in the Illinois when the big river gets too warm.

The Illinois travels a northwesterly course from its headwater forks in California, through the town of Cave Junction, to its eventual confluence with the Lower Rogue across the river from Agness. Along its lengthy course, the Illinois journeys through the northern extent of the Kalmiopsis Wilderness, where no road access is available.

The Lower Illinois, above and below Oak Flats, provides an outstanding opportunity for half-pounders between late August and late October, with the peak generally occurring from mid-September to mid-October. During low-flow winters, good fishing extends into January, with November typically being one of the best times. The Illinois River's native winter steelhead arrive between December and April, though the season closes March 31. Among them are some giants approaching 20 pounds or more.

The lower reach, from the Kalmiopsis Wilderness boundary down to the Rogue some eight miles below, is popular for both half-pounders and for the big winter natives. A drift boat can be launched off gravel bars at Oak Flats to make the drift down to the Rogue at Agness; the take-out is on Cougar Lane at the confluence. Oak Flat Road (Route 450) turns south off the Rogue River Road (FR33 from Gold Beach) just east of the Illinois River Bridge. The road leads up to Indian Creek Campground and a rough launch.

Above the Kalmiopsis Wilderness, through which the Illinois flows for about 25 miles, the river is again accessible by road. Private property makes for difficult access from Cave Junction down to the national forest boundary near the Babyfoot Lake Road (FR4201), below which access is generally good. Forest Road 4103 follows the northeast bank of the river for about 15 miles Briggs Creek. This is the most popular reach for fly fishing during the winter steelhead run as it is easily reached from Grants Pass, just 20 miles to the northeast via Hwy. 199 (turn right on County Route 5070 when you reach Selma).

With bank access good along the Illinois, anglers have little need to risk their lives trying to float the river above or through the wilderness. White-water enthusiasts are becoming more common and you wouldn't be wrong in questioning their sanity.

March is the best month for fishing the Cave Junction to Briggs Creek reach. By then the winter fish have arrived in sufficient numbers. Among them are some true giants of 20 pounds or more. This is largely a rough-and-tumble river but one conducive to a variety of techniques. The river's tailouts and cobble runs are perfectly suited to swinging a large Spey-style fly; the boulder-strewn runs and rock-gardens are perhaps better fished with a Comet or similar weighted fly. The Illinois is also a rather physical river, where you have ample opportunity to clamber over boulders and spiked wading boots or sandals should be considered mandatory.

Applegate River

The Applegate River joins the Rogue just west of Grants Pass after a somewhat leisurely journey down from the Siskiyous south of Medford and Ashland. The Applegate offers a fair run of winter steelhead between January and April, with the best fishing usually from late February through the season closure at the end of March. Steelhead numbers have been down substantially in recent years, but this small river offers good fly-fishing opportunities when runs are strong.

Applegate Dam forms the upriver boundary of the fishery, but most of the pressure is concentrated below the Little Applegate. Access is good along a network of county roads and from Hwy. 238, which turns west out of Medford, picks up the Applegate near the little village of Ruch and follows the middle reach of the river all the way northwest to Murphy. On the north bank, opposite the highway, North Applegate Road runs a parallel course from the town of Applegate up to Murphy.

The lower reach of the Applegate is accessible from Grants Pass: Follow Hwy. 238 south a short distance to a right turn at New Hope Road and then at New Hope turn west on Fish Hatchery Road, which crosses the river above the county park and swings westerly above the south bank before catching up with Hwy. 199 (Redwood Highway) out of Grants Pass. Between New Hope and Murphy, the best access is from the Southside Road.

Coquille River

The Coquille River and its forks drain an expansive area south and west of Coos Bay. Its several forks converge by the time the river reaches Myrtle Point and from there the river makes its way to the ocean at Bandon. Below its forks, the Coquille is largely a boat fishery for plunkers and trollers. Of more interest to fly anglers are the forks themselves, which receive runs of wild and hatchery winter steelhead and offer good fishing for wild cutthroat trout in their upper reaches. If the 1996 regulation mandating catch-and-release of trout on all coastal streams can hold up over time, fly anglers can expect to find increasingly excellent opportunities for native trout on the forks of the Coquille.

Generally, the South Fork Coquille offers the best winter steelhead fishing, with the run peaking between late December and early March. The South Fork is road-accessible for most of its length south of Myrtle Point, although a 12-mile reach from Milepost 4 on Powers-Agnus Road up to Coquille Falls is closed to all fishing to protect spawning salmonids. Thus the fishery essentially extends from the mouth of the South Fork at Myrtle Point upstream to the Siskiyou National Forest boundary. Access is good at points where the road parallels the river; otherwise be sure to ask permission to cross private lands.

The South Fork is the only fork of the Coquille that is easily floated. Three ramps are located above and below the town of Powers: Two miles south (upstream) of town, the city owns a gravel ramp at Orchard Park;

ODFW has a gravel ramp at Baker Creek two miles downstream of Powers and a pole slide at Beaver Creek six miles downstream of Powers. The short floats allow you to cover lots of good fly water in the course of a day.

The East Fork and North Fork Coquille both offer fair opportunity for winter steelhead, with the timing of the run about the same as for the South Fork and the other forks. The East Fork joins the North Fork a few miles northeast of Myrtle Point at the little village of Gravelford and then the North Fork reaches the main river just north of Myrtle Point. To access either fork, turn east on Myrtle Point-Sitkum Road about a mile north of Myrtle Point. When you reach Gravelford, stay right to follow the East Fork or left to follow the North Fork. The North Fork is also accessible from the Coquille-Fairview Road leading east off Hwy. 42 from Coquille.

The Middle Fork Coquille offers fair trout fishing and only marginal steelhead opportunities. It originates in the Camas Valley southwest of Roseburg and joins the main fork at Myrtle Point. Hwy. 42 follows the Middle Fork for most of its length, providing an opportunity for anglers to view clear-cutting on the most massive scale imaginable: If there stands an old-growth conifer along the Middle Fork, I apparently haven't seen it.

Pistol River

A small, rugged river, the Pistol flows through a precipitous canyon before reaching the Pacific south of Gold Beach. A lean, but fishable run of native winter steelhead enters the Pistol between December and March and sea-run cutthroat enter the river after its bar-bound mouth is breached by rain-swollen fall flows. Also, during years when the half-pounders are abundant on the Rogue, quite a few strays end up in the Pistol by mid- to late autumn.

Though fly anglers are a rare sight here during the winter, the Pistol does offer some decent fly water. Its middle reaches, dominated by pocket water, probably afford the best opportunity, but only for those willing to clamber over rugged terrain and negotiate steep embankments. County Road 690 (North Bank Pistol River Road) follows most of the lower river, but above that you must negotiate a network of logging roads and trails. Be sure to check on gate closures and obtain a copy of the Siskiyou National Forest Map (most of the river flows through lands owned by private timber companies).

Sixes River

The Sixes River meets the Pacific at Cape Blanco after a due-west plunge from the west slope of the coast mountains. This small river offers native winter steelhead and sea-run cutthroat. The steelhead runs begin

Oregon's southwest zone is known for its steelhead.

between late November and early December, peaking between mid-January and late March. The cutthroat run begins after the fall freshets in late August and continues into October with best fishing in the lower river.

The Sixes, like the other southwest coast streams, is primarily the domain of hardware and bait anglers, whose methods are better suited to high flows of winter. However, the Sixes does offer good fly water for anglers who time their outings to coincide with dry periods between January and March. Above the highway, good fly water awaits those who can avoid the gear fishermen. You can launch a boat at Edson Creek and drift down to the take-out at the Hwy. 101 Bridge behind the Sixes Grange Hall: turn off the highway at the Sixes Store immediately north of the highway bridge, then drive south past the store and behind the Grange Hall, where a narrow gravel road leads down to the unimproved (but easy) gravel bar launch.

Edson Creek Launch (earthen) lies along Sixes River Road about four miles up from Hwy. 101. Another launch, called "Mid-Drift" is located about a mile and a half downriver. The steep Edson Creek ramp requires a four-wheel-drive vehicle. Camping is available at Edson Park across the road from the ramp.

Road access is available in a few places along the river upstream from Hwy. 101, but pull-outs are few and far between. Below Hwy. 101, bank access is essentially unavailable, but the four-mile drift from 101 down to the take-out at Cape Blanco State Park takes you through some nice fly water and is an easy day-trip with good gravel-bar launches at both ends. To reach the take-out at the state park, follow Hwy. 101 south from the river and turn west on a signed road.

During the latter half of the season (mid-February through late March), fly anglers might want to explore the water above Edson Creek. The river is open up to the confluence of the South Fork at river mile 18. Sixes River Campground (BLM) is located at the confluence, offering access to about a half mile of public river frontage. Otherwise, most of the Sixes River runs through private land, making a drift boat the optimal choice.

The lower river, below Hwy. 101, is best for sea-run cutthroat. You can launch a boat at Cape Blanco State Park to fish tidewater after the first freshets. Or you can drop a boat or canoe in at the Hwy. 101 bridge and make the trek down to the state park.

Elk River

Though lightly fished by fly anglers, the Elk River near Port Orford typically offers a strong run of native winter steelhead, with peak fishing from late December through March. Like the Sixes, the Elk runs primarily through private land, so a boat offers the best access. The put-in is at the ODFW fish hatchery about nine miles east of Hwy. 101 on Elk River Road. The take-out is an earthen ramp on an ODFW access site called Iron Head, just east of the Hwy. 101 Bridge.

Sea-run cutthroat enter the Elk in the fall, after a few good rain storms. The fishing begins after the beach breaches in late September or October. You can access the mouth of the river from the beach or you can boat down from, and then struggle back up to, Iron Head. Otherwise, ask permission to access the lower river on foot from the north bank (McKenzie Road).

The upper reaches of the Elk River offer good catch-and-release fishing for wild, resident cutthroat trout. Above the fish hatchery, Siskiyou National Forest property predominates and Forest Road 5325 parallels the river all the way up to Laird Lake Campground on the South Fork. The trout-fishing holds throughout the summer and early fall, although low water during late summer concentrates many of the fish in the deeper, shaded pools.

Chetco River

The most productive south coast stream for winter steelhead, the popular and scenic Chetco runs a 50-odd-mile course from its headwaters in the Kalmiopsis Wilderness to its mouth at Brookings. For many years, fly anglers from California have converged on the Chetco during fall to pursue chinook salmon. Along the way, they earned a reputation of being a rather unruly lot, lining up prams side by side in the popular salmon holes and treating newcomers with nastiness. The pram fishery continues to this day, but not to the extent to which it did when the chinook runs were huge.

The Chetco's winter steelhead comprise its best fishery, for my money at least. The steelhead, both native and hatchery, arrive by December and continue entering the river through mid-spring. Some of the popular drift-fishing areas, including Redwood, Nook and Moller Bars, offer ideal fly water, with clean gravel bottoms predominating. March is the best month for fly anglers: gear fishermen have dispersed somewhat, water temperatures are a little warmer and a few days of dry weather creates ideal low-water conditions.

County Route 784 follows the north bank while Route 808 leads up the south side of the Chetco. Primary access is from the former. Bank access is difficult on the lower river, but about seven miles above Hwy. 101, Alfred Loeb State Park provides access to almost a mile of good water. A short distance above Loeb is the national forest boundary so access improves all the way up to South Fork at mile 16 (the uppermost launch).

The Chetco is a good drift boat river with few hazards. Most of the launches are undeveloped gravel put-ins. These include South Fork, Redwood Bar, Nook Bar, Miller Bar, Ice Box and Loeb, respectively, going downriver. Social Security Bar is a concrete launch located three miles east of Brookings.

Sea-run cutthroat enter the river between mid-August and mid-October, typically in decent numbers. The lower river, from Loeb to Brookings, is best.

Winchuck River

The little-known Winchuck River flows into the Pacific south of Brookings, just half a mile from the California border. In decades past, fly anglers used prams and drift boats to fish for chinook, but a no-boats regulation is now in effect on this small stream. The chinook salmon run remains, but the fish are difficult to pursue in the lower river without the help of a boat. However, the Winchuck does offer a run of native winter steelhead that begin to enter the river during December. The run peaks in January for hardware anglers, but March probably offers the best fly-angling opportunity.

ODFW biologist Russ Stauff says that "there is little or no fly fishing for winter steelhead" occurring on the Winchuck in recent years, despite the stream's potential. Stauff recommends the reach from the Siskiyou National Forest Boundary up to Wheeler Creek (above which the river is closed to fishing). This two-mile stretch is easily accessed via Curry County Route 896/FR1108, which turns west off Hwy. 101 a mile north of the California border. Below the USFS boundary, the Winchuck flows through private property, but the road follows close to the stream in places. Be sure to ask permission to cross private lands.

Hunter Creek

Hunter Creek is a small stream located just south of Gold Beach. Hwy. 101 crosses its mouth just north of Buena Vista State Park. Native winter steelhead ascend the creek between December and March, although the creek is closed until January 1. ODFW biologist Russ Stauff says, "I've never seen a fly fisherman on Hunter Creek (but) I'd recommend the upper reaches, above the South Fork."

KEN MORRISH PHOTO

Curry County Route 635 follows the creek, crossing the South Fork. After that, some bushwhacking through steep, rugged country is required to reach the next several miles of river. Route 635 becomes FR3680, which again reaches the river several miles above the South Fork. Be sure to obtain a copy of the Siskiyou National Forest Map before venturing out.

Diamond Lake

This large scenic lake has long been a destination for many Oregon anglers. Diamond Lake sits at 5,100 feet in the heart of the Cascade range, with the stark pinnacles of 9,182-foot Mt. Thielson dominating one horizon and 8,363-foot Mt. Bailey the other. The former peak is one of the most rugged and beautiful mountains in the Oregon Cascades.

Rainbows are the attraction in this sprawling, fertile lake and trout of two to four pounds are typical during a good year, despite the fact that Diamond Lake is managed as a general-regulations water. Trollers work the lake day in and day out through the season, as does a substantial crowd of worm-drowners and Powerbaiters. They all take their share of the trout, but so to do the fly anglers who work the near-shore shallows by boat or float tube.

A fair hatch of *Callibaetis* mayflies occurs during the summer and Chironomids hatch from ice-out through autumn, with the early and late-season hatches being most significant. Otherwise, wet flies and streamers will prove successful most of the time.

Diamond Lake is easily reached via Hwy. 138 (North Umpqua Highway). Follow the highway west from Hwy. 97 or east from Roseburg and watch for the signs near the top of the pass. Three campgrounds and a resort are located on the lake, which is encircled by Forest Road 4795.

Lemolo Lake

This 400-acre reservoir on the upper North Umpqua system offers fair fishing for brown trout that can reach several pounds. The best fishing occurs early and late (June and again in the fall) because the reservoir is drawn down substantially by midsummer. Float-tubers can fish the Lake Creek and North Umpqua arms, where trout concentrate. Brook trout are available as well. Several campgrounds are located at Lemolo. The most direct access to the lake is from Forest Road 2610, which turns north off Hwy. 138 about nine miles northwest of Diamond Lake Junction.

Toketee Reservoir

Like Lemolo Lake, Toketee Reservoir offers fair to good fishing for brown trout that can reach impressive sizes. the best fishing occurs in the spring, from March through May, and again in the fall. The reservoir lies just to the north of Hwy. 138, some 25 miles west of Diamond Lake Junction and about 40 miles east of Glide. The turn-off is clearly marked.

Mainstem Umpqua River

The mainstem Umpqua and a substantial length of the South Umpqua comprise one of Oregon's most productive smallmouth bass fisheries. Virtually throughout the mainstem, smallmouth abound in surprising density. During summer and early fall, when the river runs low and clear, fly anglers can catch bass by the dozens. Small fish are the rule, with six- to 12-inch specimens about average; 12- to 14-inch bass are fairly common. An occasional three- to five-pound bass shows up, but these aren't caught with any regularity.

John Shewey with a south coast winter steelhead.

A boat or float tube goes a long way towards improving your fishing on this large river. Tubers should confine themselves to the more placid reaches as the Mainstem Umpqua includes some rough water. The bass are distributed throughout the system, at least as far down river as Scottsburg. Popular reaches include the lengthy, meandering stretch from Yellow Creek down to Elkton, which is accessible at a few spots along Hwy. 138 and from several secondary roads following the river in various places. Get a good map before trying to figure out all the secondary roads. Popular accesses below Elkton include Sawyer Rapids and Scotts Creek, both of which include lots of good water, especially if you float between the two.

Further downriver, from Scottsburg to Winchester Bay, the Umpqua boasts a late spring run of striped bass, some of which reach 40 or more pounds. They aren't easy to catch, owing to their spotty distribution through widespread habitat, but they are well worth pursuit if stripers turn your crank. During summer and early fall, the stripers can be found cruising flats and channels in Winchester Bay. You will need a boat and a largely nocturnal lifestyle, but fishing these brutes in the bay can create some serious excitement for those who devote some time to figuring out the movement pattern of the fish in conjunction with the tides.

Selected Fly Patterns for Oregon Waters

Winter Steelhead Flies

Spawning Winter Purple (John Shewey)

Hook: Heavy wire salmon hook, size 4/0-4
Tag: Flat silver tinsel
Body: Fluorescent hot pink floss
Wings: Five marabou "spikes," first two of hot pink or cerise, last three deep purple
Hackle: Purple
Cheeks: Jungle cock
Collar: Guinea dyed cerise or purple

Boss Comet

Tag: Flat or oval silver
Tail: Black bucktail or similar
Body: Black chenille
Rib: Silver
Hackle: Red
Eyes: Large silver bead chain

Hot Orange Comet

Tag: Gold
Tail: Hot orange bucktail
Body: Gold Diamond Braid and/or orange chenille
Rib: Gold or silver, through chenille
Hackle: Hot orange
Eyes: Large bead chain

Orange Heron (Syd Glasso)

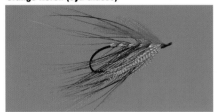

Tag: Flat silver tinsel, optional
Body: 2/3 orange silk, 1/3 orange seal dubbing or substitute
Rib: Flat silver and small oval silver
Hackle: Gray heron substitute (blue-eared pheasant) through body
Throat: Teal flank
Wing: Four orange hackles

General Practitioner

Tag: Gold
Tail: Orange bucktail or similar and a single golden pheasant tippet feather with center removed, tied in flat to represent pincers
Body: Orange wool or dubbing
Rib: Gold oval
Hackle: Orange saddle, palmered
Wing: Golden pheasant flank feathers, tied flat over top as shellback

Skunk

Tag: Silver
Tail: Red
Body: Black chenille, wool or dubbing
Rib: Silver
Hackle: Black
Wing: White

Polar Shrimp

Tag: Silver
Tail: Orange hackle fibers
Body: Fluorescent orange chenille
Hackle: Fluorescent orange
Wing: White
Cheeks: Jungle cock, optional

Sea-run Cutthroat Flies

Borden Special (Robert Borden)

Hook: Bronze or nickel wet-fly hook, size 4-8
Tail: Mix of yellow and hot pink hackle fibers
Body: Hot pink rabbit dubbing
Rib: Flat silver
Wing: White arctic fox tail
Hackle: Yellow then hot pink

Alsea Special

Tag: Gold
Tail: Pink and orange hackle fibers
Body: Coral pink chenille or dubbing
Rib: Gold
Wing: White arctic fox or polar bear
Hackle: Coral pink or orange/pink mixed

Purple Joe

Tag: Silver
Tail: Red hackle fibers
Butt: Fluorescent hot orange wool or floss
Body: Purple sparkle chenille
Wings: Badger hackles, splayed
Hackle: Badger

Dark Spruce

Tail: Peacock sword
Body: 1/2 red floss, 1/2 peacock herl
Rib: Fine oval gold
Wings: Dark furnace hackles
Hackle: Dark furnace

Jim Cope Lake Flies

Jim Cope, who resides in LaPine, has long been known for his beautifully crafted and exceptionally productive stillwater flies. His dressings were designed for and used most extensively on the lakes of Central Oregon's Century Drive, including Davis Lake, Crane Prairie Reservoir and Hosmer Lake. Among Jim's many unique ideas is his use of both synthetic and natural paintbrush bristles to make ribs and wing pads on his flies. These bristles have proven far more durable than many of the traditional materials, such as pheasant tail fibers and turkey tail fibers. For those who do not tie, Jim's flies are available at a number of different fly shops, including several in Central Oregon.

Cope Callibaetis Emerger

Hook: Mustad 3906B, size 12-16
Tail: Dark mottled coastal deer hair, stacked and tied short
Body: Gray-brown rabbit dubbing (or to match natural)
Rib: Fine copper wire
Wing: Coastal deer hair tied as a short tuft on the top half of the fly

Cope Callibaetis Nymph

Hook: 2XL nymph hook, size 12-14
Tail: Natural lemon wood duck fibers
Body: Same as above (to match naturals)
Rib: 8 wraps dyed-brown synthetic paintbrush bristle
Wingcase: Dyed brown synthetic paintbrush bristles
Thorax: Same as body
Legs: 4-5 wood duck fibers per side

Cope Siphlonurus Nymph

Hook: 2XL nymph hook, size 10-14
Tail: Gray hackle fibers
Body: Gray rabbit dubbing
Rib: Brown paintbrush bristle
Wingcase: Gray paintbrush bristles
Thorax: Same as body
Legs: Gray hackle fibers

Cope Eyed Damsel, Olive

Hook: Tiemco Size 200 or similar, size 8-12
Tail & Legs: Dyed-olive pheasant tail fibers
Body: Olive rabbit dubbing to match natural
Rib: Medium olive-dyed paintbrush bristle
Wingpad: Dyed-olive boar's hair paintbrush bristles
Eyes: Melted mono eyes painted black
Head/Thorax: Olive rabbit dubbing (same as body)

Cope Eyed Damsel, Brown

Hook: Tiemco Size 200 or similar, size 10-12
Tail & Legs: Natural brown pheasant tail fibers
Body: Light brown rabbit dubbing
Rib: Brown-dyed paintbrush bristle
Wingpad: Dyed-brown boar's hair paintbrush bristles
Eyes: Melted mono eyes painted black
Thorax/Head: Same as body

Cope Wingcase Damsel

Hook: Tiemco size 200, size 8-12
Tail: Dyed-green guinea fibers
Body: Olive green hare's ear dubbing
Rib: Fine flat gold tinsel
Wingcase: Peacock herl
Thorax: Olive green hare's ear dubbing, picked out
Legs: Dyed-green guinea fibers

J.C. Damsel

Hook: Tiemco #200, size 12
Tail: Olive marabou tuft, pinched off to proper length
Body: Medium olive rabbit dubbing
Rib: Light olive-dyed paintbrush bristle
Legs: Medium-light olive hackle fibers
Wingcase: Olive-dyed synthetic paintbrush bristles
Head: Dubbed, same as body
Eyes: Melted olive mono, unpainted

Chartreuse J.C. Damsel

Hook: Tiemco #200, size 12
Tail: Light golden-olive marabou, pinched off to proper length
Body: Light golden-olive rabbit dubbing
Rib: Olive-dyed paintbrush bristle
Legs: Light olive hackle fibers
Wingcase: Light olive-dyed synthetic paintbrush bristles
Head: Dubbed, same as body
Eyes: Melted olive mono, unpainted

Cope Prairie Damsel

Hook: 3XL nymph/streamer, size 6-10
Tail: Dyed-yellow-olive grizzly hackle fibers
Body: Medium/light olive dubbing
Rib: 8 turns dyed-olive flat monofilament
Collar: Dyed-olive grizzly hackle
Head: Dubbed, same as body

Cope Dragon Fly Nymph

Hook: 3XL streamer/nymph, size 6-8
Underbody: Flattened wool or dubbing
Tail: Speckled hen back fibers
Body: A mix of brown mink, brown rabbit, sable and golden-brown rabbit to arrive at shade of natural, or other colors to match particular dragonfly nymphs
Rib: Brown thread, reversed
Legs: Tufts of speckled hen back fibers
Wingcase: Brown-dyed boar's hair paintbrush bristles
Eyes: Melted monofilament eyes
Head: Dubbed, same as body

Cope Wood Duck Damsel

Hook: 3XL streamer/nymph, size 8-12
Tail: Wood duck fibers
Rib: Dyed-olive synthetic paintbrush bristle
Body: Blend of black, yellow and olive rabbit to arrive at color of natural
Hackle: Olive-dyed grizzly
Head: Dubbed, same as body

Cope Sidewinder

Hook: Standard length straight-eye wet fly, size 10-12
Tail: Marabou tip fibers, tied long
Body: Olive or light olive rabbit dubbing
Wingpad: Natural boar's hair paintbrush bristles
Legs: Olive-dyed hackle fibers
Eyes: Melted olive mono, unpainted

Selected John Shewey Stillwater Flies for Oregon Lakes and Reservoirs

Shewey's Damsel

Hook: *2XL nymph, size 8-12*
Tail: *Marabou fluff*
Body: *Marabou fibers wrapped on shank*
Rib: *Fine wire*
Thorax: *Marabou fibers wrapped on shank*
Legs: *Partridge dyed light green*
Wingcase: *Lemon wood duck*

Diving Damsel

Tail: *Marabou*
Body: *Marabou*
Rib: *Fine wire*
Legs: *Partridge hackle, dyed green*
Head: *Metal bead*

Strip Damsel

Hook: *2XL or 3XL*
Tail: *Sparse tuft of rabbit strip fur*
Body: *Seal dubbing to match natural*
Eyes: *Melted mono eyes*

Sleeze Leech

Hook: *Streamer, size 2-6*
Tail: *A few strands of Krystal Flash*
Body: *Dubbed fur, seal or similar*
Wing: *Thin rabbit strip, tied down fore and aft*

Nevada Leech

Hook: *Streamer, size 1/0-4*
Tail: *A few strands of Krystal Flash and a rabbit strip*
Body: *Mohair yarn*
Head: *Spun rabbit hair*

Thin-water Leech

Hook: *Streamer, size 2-10*
Tail: *Marabou, sparse*
Body: *Dubbed, sparse and picked out*
Rib: *Fine wire, optional*

Super Scud

Hook: *2XL wet fly, size 10-16*
Shellback: *Mix of wood duck and Krystal Flash*
Body: *Rabbit dubbing, loop-dubbed onto Krystal Flash and picked out*
Rib: *Fine wire*

Bloodworm Larvae

Hook: *2XL light wire, size 12-18*
Body: *Pheasant tail dyed crimson*
Rib: *Fine wire*
Head: *Fine peacock herl*

Bloodworm Pupa

Hook: *2XL light wire, size 12-18*
Body: *Pheasant tail dyed crimson*
Rib: *Fine wire*
Gills: *White Antron*
Head: *Fine peacock herl*
Wingcase: *Pheasant tail fibers, dyed crimson*

Bloodworm Emerger

Hook: *2XL light wire, size 12-18*
Body: *Pheasant tail dyed crimson*
Rib: *Fine wire*
Head: *Fine peacock herl and foam bubble to float the fly*

Callibaetis Krystal Spinner

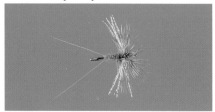

Tails: *Micro Fibetts, divided*
Body: *Light gray-tan dubbing*
Wings: *A few strands of Krystal Flash (pearl) tied spent*
Hackle: *Grizzly, wrapped through wings and over dubbed thorax, clipped flush below*
Head: *Same as body*

Selected Trout Dry Flies for Oregon Streams

Elk Hair Caddis

Body: Dubbed fur
Hackle: Grizzly or to match body
Wing: Elk hair

X-Caddis

Tail: Z-lon as trailing shuck
Body: Dubbed fur to match natural
Wing: Deer hair, tied short

October Caddis

Body: Orange dubbing
Hackle: Brown, reverse palmered over body
Rib: Fine wire
Wing: Deer or elk, with butt ends left for head
Collar: Brown and grizzly hackle mixed

Maxwell's Jughead

Tail: Deer or elk, stacked and tied short
Body: Orange or yellow yarn
Hackle: Brown, palmered and clipped short
Wing/Head: Spun deer hair

Royal Wulff

Tail: Mouse hair or elk mane
Body: Peacock herl, divided by a band of red floss
Wings: White calf tail or body
Hackle: Brown

Stimulator

Tail: Dark elk hair
Body: Yellow or orange rabbit dubbing
Hackle: Furnace, palmered through body
Rib: Fine wire
Wing: Elk hair
Collar: Grizzly hackle palmered through orange dubbing

Humpy

Tail: Elk hock or moose mane
Shellback: Elk hock or moose mane
Body: Thread, floss or wool
Wings: Natural elk or white calf tail
Hackle: Grizzly/brown mixed

Parachute Adams

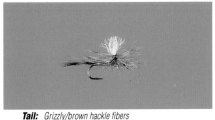

Tail: Grizzly/brown hackle fibers
Body: Gray dubbing
Wing: Post of white calf tail or Antron yarn
Hackle: Mixed brown and grizzly

Light Cahill

Tail: Light ginger hackle fibers
Body: Light cream dubbing
Wings: Lemon wood duck
Hackle: Light ginger

Compara-dun

Tails: Micro Fibetts or hackle fibers, divided
Body: Dubbing to match natural
Wing: Deer hair

Sparkle Dun

Tail: Z-lon tied as trailing shuck
Body: Dubbing to match natural
Wing: Deer hair

CDC Mayfly Dun

Tails: Micro Fibetts or hackle fibers, divided
Body: Dubbing to match natural
Wing: CDC plumes bunched and clipped

CDC Mayfly Emerger

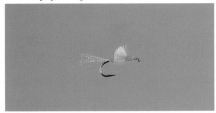

Tail: Z-lon or similar tied as trailing shuck
Body: Dubbing to match natural
Wing: CDC plumes bunched and clipped short

Selected Trout Nymphs/Wet Flies for Oregon Waters

Brook's Stonefly Nymph

Tail: Black goose biots
Body: Black wool yarn
Rib: Copper wire
Hackle: Mixed grizzly and brown, wrapped over thorax

Golden Stonefly Nymph

Tail: Tan goose biots
Body: Amber rabbit or seal dubbing
Rib: Copper wire
Wingpad: Turkey tail
Thorax: Same as body, picked out

Gold Ribbed Hare's Ear Nymph

Tag: Flat gold tinsel (optional)
Tail: Rabbit mask fur or partridge fibers
Body: Hare's ear dubbing
Rib: Gold oval tinsel
Wingpad: Turkey tail or wing segment
Thorax: Same as body

Pheasant Tail Nymph

Tail: Ring-necked pheasant tail fibers
Body: Ring-necked pheasant tail fibers
Rib: Fine gold wire
Wingpad/legs: Ring-necked pheasant tail fibers
Thorax: Peacock herl

Peeking Caddis

Body: Natural tan or dark gray rabbit dubbing, loop-dubbed or ribbed with fine gold oval
Thorax: Green or cream dubbing
Collar: Partridge
Head: Black ostrich

Green Rockworm

Body: Fine green wool or dubbing (loop-dubbed)
Legs: Partridge fibers
Head: Black dubbing, peacock herl or black ostrich

Zug Bug

Tail: Peacock sword
Body: Peacock herl
Rib: Fine gold or silver oval
Legs: Brown hackle fibers or partridge hackle
Wingpad: Lemon wood duck, clipped

Woolly Bugger

Tail: Marabou
Body: Chenille, dubbing or herl
Hackle: Saddle hackle, reverse-palmered through body
Rib: Fine wire

Peacock Carey

Tail: Natural pheasant rump fibers
Body: Peacock herl
Collar: Natural pheasant rump fibers

Partridge & Orange

Hook: Wet fly, size 8-16
Body: Orange silk
Collar: Two turns of natural tan dubbing (optional) then two turns of natural partridge hackle

FEDERATION OF FLY FISHERS FLY PATTERN ENCYCLOPEDIA
Over 1600 of the Best Fly Patterns
Edited by Al & Gretchen Beatty

Simply stated, this book is a Federation of Fly Fishers' conclave taken to the next level, a level that allows the reader to enjoy the learning and sharing in the comfort of their own home. The flies, ideas, and techniques shared herein are from the "best of the best" demonstration fly tiers North America has to offer. The tiers are the famous as well as the unknown with one simple characteristic in common; they freely share their knowledge. Many of the unpublished patterns in this book contain materials, tips, tricks, or gems of information never before seen.

As you leaf through these pages, you will get from them just what you would if you spent time in the fly tying area at any FFF function. At such a show, if you dedicate time to observing the individual tiers, you can learn the information, tips, or tricks they are demonstrating. All of this knowledge can be found in *Federation of Fly Fishers Fly Pattern Encyclopedia* so get comfortable and get ready to improve upon your fly tying technique with the help of some of North America's best fly tiers. Full color, 8 1/2 x 11 inches, 232 pages.

SB: $39.95   SPIRAL HB: $49.95

THE FLY TIER'S BENCHSIDE REFERENCE TO TECHNIQUES AND DRESSING STYLES
Ted Leeson and Jim Schollmeyer

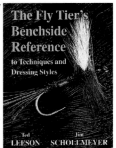

Printed in full color on top-quality paper, this book features over **3,000 color photographs and over 400,000 words** describing and showing, step-by-step, hundreds of fly-tying techniques! Leeson and Schollmeyer have collaborated to produce this masterful volume which will be the standard fly-tying reference book for the entire trout-fishing world. Through enormous effort on their part they bring to all who love flies and fly fishing a wonderful compendium of fly-tying knowledge. Every fly tier should have this book in their library! All color, 8 1/2 by 11 inches, 464 pages, over 3,000 color photographs, index, hardbound with dust jacket.
HARDBOUND: $100.00

TROUT FLIES OF THE WEST: CONTEMPORARY PATTERNS FROM THE ROCKY MOUNTAINS & WEST
Jim Schollmeyer and Ted Leeson

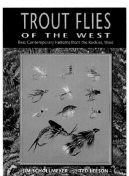

This beautifully illustrated, all-color book features over 300 of the West's best specialty trout flies and their recipes and an explanation of each fly's use. The flies and information were researched from scores of the West's finest fly shops. Over 600 color photographs. The very latest word on the most effective Western patterns! 8 1/2 x 11, 128 pages.
Softbound: $34.95
Spiral Hardbound: $44.95

STEELHEADER'S REFERENCE GUIDE
Steelhead Catch Information Statistics for Determining Where and When to Catch Oregon and Washington Steelhead
Eldon Ladd

This thoroughly researched report/book has complete steelhead catch statistics for Oregon and Washington streams and rivers documented by month. Hundreds of waters are included, as well as Columbia River dam counts on a monthly basis back to 1938. By using it you can guarantee that you are fishing the right river at the right time for either winter- or summer-run steelhead! Smolt releases for all streams are also included as well for the last 10 years. The information in this report is invaluable for understanding steelhead runs and where the best fishing occurs year after year. 100 pages, 8 1/2 x 11 inches.
SPIRAL: $19.95

FRONTIER FLIES:
PATTERNS ON THE CUTTING EDGE
Troy Bachmann
Photographed by Jim Schollmeyer.

Features the finest and most contemporary flies to tie and fish. All-color fly pattern book with over 600 cutting-edge flies (with dressings and fishing explanations) for virtually all sport-fishing situations. Also, narrative by Rick Hafele, Mark Bachmann, Dave Hughes, Bill McMillan, Tom Earnhardt, Brian O'Keefe. 8 1/2 by 11 inches, 128 pages.
Softbound: $29.95

WESTERN STREAMSIDE GUIDE:
RECOGNIZING THE NATURAL, SELECTING ITS IMITATION
(Fully Revised Edition)
Dave Hughes

This is a fully revised, all-color, new edition of one of the classics on Western trout fishing. Filled with everything you need to know about the hatches of the West and the fly patterns to use. Both insects and fly patterns shown in full color. Compact and easy to read and carry afield, it shows you exactly what fly to use in any given situation and how best to fish it. Fly dressings included. 4 x 8 inches, 136 pages.
Softbound $15.95   Hardbound $24.95

The Fish Bum's Guide to Catching Larger Trout:
AN ILLUSTRATED MANUAL ON STILLWATER TACTICS
Michael Croft

A brilliant explanation of how to fly fish still water, ponds, lakes, and reservoirs by a long-practiced expert. You will marvel at the inside information presented in a dramatic and hilarious drawing style. Valuable information about casting, reading water, lines, reels, rods, float equipment, flies, hatches, weather, structure. Hundreds of hand-drawn illustrations. 8 1/2 x 11 inches, 96 pages.
Softbound: $14.95

FRANK AMATO PUBLICATIONS, INC.
P.O. Box 82112, Portland, OR 97282